Design and Prototyping for Drupal

D1305923

Dani Nordin

O'REILLY®

Beijing · Cambridge · Farnham · Köln · Sebastopol · Tokyo

Design and Prototyping for Drupal
by Dani Nordin

Published by O'Reilly Media, Inc., 1005 Gravenstein Highway North, Sebastopol, CA 95472.

O'Reilly books may be purchased for educational, business, or sales promotional use. Online editions are also available for most titles (*http://my.safaribooksonline.com*). For more information, contact our corporate/institutional sales department: (800) 998-9938 or *corporate@oreilly.com*.

Editors:	Julie Steele and Meghan Blanchette	**Cover Designer:**	Karen Montgomery
Production Editor:	Kristen Borg	**Interior Designer:**	David Futato
Proofreader:	O'Reilly Production Services	**Illustrator:**	Robert Romano

Revision History for the First Edition:
    2011-12-13   First release
See *http://oreilly.com/catalog/errata.csp?isbn=9781449305505* for release details.

ISBN: 978-1-449-30550-5

[LSI]

1323795289

Table of Contents

Preface

Introduction

If you're reading this book, you're probably a web designer who has heard of Drupal, wants to get started with it, and may have even tried it out a couple of times. And you might be frustrated because even if you're used to code, Drupal has thrown you a major learning curve that you hadn't expected. And just when you think you've gotten a basic site together, now you have to figure out how to make it *look* right—and the whole process starts over again.

Yep, I've been there too. That's why I wrote this book.

This book is for the solo site builder or small team that's itching to do interesting things with Drupal, but needs a bit of help understanding how to set up a successful Drupal project. It's for the designer who knows HTML and CSS, but doesn't want to have to learn how to speak developer in order to parse Drupal documentation. Most importantly, this book is for those who want to use Drupal to make their vision a reality, but need help working their minds around the way that Drupal handles design challenges.

What I present here are not recipes for specific use cases; although recipes can be useful, experience has shown there's rarely just one way to accomplish an objective in Drupal. Rather, what I'm offering is context: a way of understanding what Drupal is and how it works, so that you can get over the hump and start figuring things out on your own. Over the course of this series of books, I'll help you understand:

- How to plan and manage Drupal projects successfully (in the *Planning and Managing Drupal Projects* guide)
- How to more effectively create visual design for Drupal by understanding what Drupal is spitting out (in *Design and Prototyping for Drupal*)
- How to break down your design layouts to turn them into Drupal themes (in *Design and Prototyping for Drupal*)
- How to get started with version control, Drush, and other ninja-developer Drupal Magick that can make your life much easier working with Drupal (in *Drupal Development Tricks for Designers*)

In This Volume

In this second volume, *Design and Prototyping for Drupal*, we'll start digging into the practical design challenges that Drupal presents, and look at some strategies for dealing with them. You will learn:

- Strategies for sketching, wireframing and designing effective layouts for Drupal
- How to break down a Drupal layout to understand its basic components, and where those components are coming from within Drupal
- An introduction to working with layout grids and the 960 grid system to facilitate efficient wireframing, layout and theming
- The basics of Drupal's theming layer, including what to look for in a base theme, and how to create a subtheme to hold your customizations
- Strategies for managing the markup that Drupal produces, including the markup that comes from Views, the powerful module that helps organize and display the content in your Drupal site
- An introduction to LessCSS, which can help you organize your CSS and theme your site more efficiently

A Quick Note on Nomenclature

Before we continue, it's important to make a distinction between *visual design* and *theming*. While many themers can design and vice versa, visual design (as defined in this guide) is the act of *creating a set of visual standards* that will control the way the site looks. This could involve something as simple as picking out colors and font choices for the site, and creating some standards for laying out type, boxes, etc. More often, it involves creating visual mockups in a program such as Fireworks or Photoshop.

Theming, on the other hand, is the process of implementing those visual standards across the site's template files, using HTML, CSS, and PHP. While theming can (and sometimes does) happen without visual design, design is what truly brings the message home to the client's audience. When well constructed, and implemented by talented themers, a site's visual design is an important factor in whether the site meets the client's business objectives.

Theming, as a distinctive job description, seems relatively unique to the Drupal universe. While many other CMSs include some idea of a theme layer—"theme" being defined as a set of customizable templates through which content is displayed—with many CMSs, designers either appropriate an existing theme to create their design, or they hand finished design comps off as either images or HTML files to a developer, who integrates those files into the website's structure. While this can also be done in Drupal, it's not advised; Drupal's theme layer has a level of complexity to it that makes simply modifying an existing theme problematic. For this reason, many Drupal designers will turn to themers, also called "Front-End Developers," to help them implement their designs, particularly if they include any kind of fancy stuff.

A Note on Code

One thing I must emphasize about the Drupal design process is that it often involves getting into code—but not always. As mentioned before, many excellent Drupal designers never touch a line of code; however, *those designers always have developers who help them implement their designs*. If you want to design for Drupal but don't have access to developers, well, you're going to need to learn code and site building in Drupal. There's no way around it if you want to do good work.

The good news, however, is that's part of what you'll learn about in this book. While I'm not going to provide you with a recipe for a generic promotional site, or guidance on how to install Drupal, what I will do is show you how I figured out some of the stickier design and implementation challenges for a couple of real world projects, which will give you an insider's look at what it's like to design and prototype in Drupal.

But Dani, I've Never Even Installed Drupal Before; What Do I Do?

This guide assumes that you're at least somewhat familiar with Drupal, particularly Drupal 7. If you've never worked with Drupal at all, you might find some of the examples confusing. If you need to get started working in Drupal from the ground up, I recommend checking out NodeOne's excellent "Learn Drupal 7" training series. The series, located at *http://nodeone.se/blogg/learn-drupal-7-sceencast-series-summed-up*, will walk you through the basics you need to get started building your own site. Don't worry; I'll wait for you.

Conventions Used in This Book

The following typographical conventions are used in this book:

Italic
> Indicates new terms, URLs, email addresses, filenames, and file extensions.

`Constant width`
> Used for program listings, as well as within paragraphs to refer to program elements such as variable or function names, databases, data types, environment variables, statements, and keywords.

`Constant width bold`
> Shows commands or other text that should be typed literally by the user.

`Constant width italic`
> Shows text that should be replaced with user-supplied values or by values determined by context.

This icon signifies a tip, suggestion, or general note.

This icon indicates a warning or caution.

Using Code Examples

This book is here to help you get your job done. In general, you may use the code in this book in your programs and documentation. You do not need to contact us for permission unless you're reproducing a significant portion of the code. For example, writing a program that uses several chunks of code from this book does not require permission. Selling or distributing a CD-ROM of examples from O'Reilly books does require permission. Answering a question by citing this book and quoting example code does not require permission. Incorporating a significant amount of example code from this book into your product's documentation does require permission.

We appreciate, but do not require, attribution. An attribution usually includes the title, author, publisher, and ISBN. For example: "*Design and Prototyping for Drupal* by Dani Nordin (O'Reilly). Copyright 2012 Dani Nordin, 978-1-449-30550-5."

If you feel your use of code examples falls outside fair use or the permission given above, feel free to contact us at *permissions@oreilly.com*.

Safari® Books Online

Safari Books Online is an on-demand digital library that lets you easily search over 7,500 technology and creative reference books and videos to find the answers you need quickly.

With a subscription, you can read any page and watch any video from our library online. Read books on your cell phone and mobile devices. Access new titles before they are available for print, and get exclusive access to manuscripts in development and post feedback for the authors. Copy and paste code samples, organize your favorites, download chapters, bookmark key sections, create notes, print out pages, and benefit from tons of other time-saving features.

O'Reilly Media has uploaded this book to the Safari Books Online service. To have full digital access to this book and others on similar topics from O'Reilly and other publishers, sign up for free at *http://my.safaribooksonline.com*.

How to Contact Us

Please address comments and questions concerning this book to the publisher:

O'Reilly Media, Inc.
1005 Gravenstein Highway North
Sebastopol, CA 95472
800-998-9938 (in the United States or Canada)
707-829-0515 (international or local)
707-829-0104 (fax)

We have a web page for this book, where we list errata, examples, and any additional information. You can access this page at:

http://oreilly.com/catalog/0636920020295

To comment or ask technical questions about this book, send email to:

bookquestions@oreilly.com

For more information about our books, courses, conferences, and news, see our website at *http://www.oreilly.com.*

Find us on Facebook: *http://facebook.com/oreilly*

Follow us on Twitter: *http://twitter.com/oreillymedia*

Watch us on YouTube: *http://www.youtube.com/oreillymedia*

About the Reviewers

Todd Ross Nienkerk, Four Kitchens co-founder, has been involved in the web design and publishing industries since 1996. As an active member of the Drupal community, Todd regularly speaks at Drupal events and participates in code sprints all over the world. As a member of the Drupal.org Redesign Team, Todd helped spearhead the effort to redesign Drupal.org and communicate a fresher, more effective Drupal brand. He is also a member of the Drupal Documentation Team and has chaired tracks for DrupalCon Copenhagen 2010, DrupalCon Chicago 2011, and DrupalCon Denver 2012. Todd is currently serving as the DrupalCon global chair for all design, user experience, and theming tracks.

Tricia Okin is a designer based and working in Brooklyn since 2001 and founded *papercut* in 2004. *papercut* was resurrected in early 2009 by Tricia after realizing she wanted to make good work with tangibility & purpose. She also realized she couldn't and would rather not do it alone in a design vacuum. From there, Tricia called on the best resources she could find and mustered up a gang of wily collaborators with as much passion for being their own bosses as she has.

For nearly two decades, **Jenifer Tidwell** has been designing and building user interfaces for a variety of industry verticals. She has experience in designing both desktop and Web applications, and currently designs and develops websites for small businesses. She recently worked on redesigning the interface for Google Books. Before that, as a user interface designer at The MathWorks, Jenifer was instrumental in a redesign of the charting and visualization UI of MATLAB, which is used by researchers, students, and engineers worldwide to develop cars, planes, proteins, and theories about the universe. Jenifer blogs about UI patterns and other design-related topics at *http://designinginterfaces.com/blog*.

Acknowledgments

To be honest, I'm still amazed at being given the chance to write this book. It had been swirling around in my mind for a while, and I consider it one of life's happier coincidences that I happened to get the opportunity to write about Drupal in not one, but two major books this year.

A brief list of thanks to the folks who have helped me in various capacities to help this book see the light of day:

My intrepid editors, Julie Steele and Meghan Blanchette, for giving me the opportunity to write the book, and for helping me make sense of O'Reilly's lengthy style guide. Also thanks to Laurel Ruma for making the introduction to Julie so I could actually *sell* this crazy idea.

Todd Nienkerk of Four Kitchens (fourkitchens.com) helped me understand how the ideas I've used in really tiny teams apply to the work of larger teams; his feedback as a reviewer (as indicated by the many times I quote him throughout this text), was invaluable.

Tricia Okin of Papercut (papercutny.com) was instrumental in helping me deconstruct what my readers would need. She also provided a tremendous real-world example for the book in the form of the *Urban Homesteaders Unite* project. Her commentary throughout this process, as well as her wicked sense of humor and willingness to actually learn Drupal, has been a constant source of awesome.

Various colleagues and professional acquaintances, in and out of the Drupal community, who were kind enough to let me interview them: Greg Segall of OnePica, Richard Banfield of Fresh Tilled Soil, David Rondeau of inContext Design, Todd Nienkerk, Jason Pamental, Amy Seals, Mike Rohde, Ryan Parsley, Leisa Reichelt and Andrew Burcin.

Claudio Luis Vera, for introducing me to Drupal, and being a mentor, collaborator, and commiserator for the last several years. Also, Ben Buckman of New Leaf Digital, who has been one of the guiding forces behind my passion to bring Drupally knowledge —particularly Drush, Git and other stuff—to my fellow designers.

Finally, I want to thank the niecelet, Patience Marie Nordin, for giving me someone to be a role model to, and my husband, Nicolas Malyska, for being the most supportive partner anyone can hope for.

PART I

Getting Started:
Some Stuff to Consider

CHAPTER 1

Design for Drupal: Basic Concepts

At the most recent Drupal Design Camp in Boston,[*] Drupal founder Dries Buytaert mentioned in his keynote speech, "I make designers write PHP. And produce horrible code. You guys should hate me."

While this announcement got a big laugh from attendees at the camp, Dries wasn't completely joking. Creating effective design for Drupal requires a willingness to acquire some technical knowledge. If you've ever thought of using Drupal as a "quick" or "cheap" way to build a website, and you've experimented with it at all, you've already learned that you were dead wrong in that assumption.

But, if you're willing to build on your design skills, learn some basic principles, and apply them to an interesting and rapidly growing technology, you might find yourself very happy working with Drupal. And believe it or not, the Drupal community will love you for it; the last couple of years in particular has seen a renaissance of talented designers who are not only doing beautiful work in Drupal, but they're showing others how to do it as well. If you want proof, look no further than the impressive collection of videos from Boston's most recent Drupal Design Camp, which you can find at *http: //ttv.mit.edu/collections/drupal:1922*.

Blatant plug for the Drupal design community aside, let's move on to some basic principles of creating design for Drupal. To recap from the *Planning and Managing Drupal Projects* guide, visual design (defined here primarily as creating the look and feel for a given site), often comes either after or alongside the technical implementation phase of a Drupal project. See Figure 1-1 for a reminder.

This is important for a couple of reasons:

1. Focusing on visual design later in the process helps clients focus on information hierarchy, content and structure in the early phases—which is especially important for content-rich or interaction-driven sites.

---

[*] *http://boston2011.design4drupal.org/*

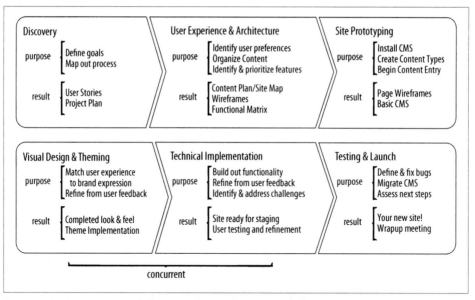

Figure 1-1. An overview of the Drupal site planning and design process. See how Technical Implementation and Visual Design go together? That's important.

2. As mentioned in the *Planning and Managing* guide, having actual content and structure for the site at least somewhat established prior to starting visual design gives you a better idea of where you're starting from—which makes it easier to create layouts that are both visually attractive and feasible to implement.

This last piece—*feasible to implement*—is one of the core challenges to working in Drupal, and where many visual designers end up going crazy. Whether we want it to or not, Drupal has ways it likes to do things—a fact that is true with any web-based framework (yes, even WordPress). By understanding and respecting how Drupal likes to do things, it's easier to develop design patterns that allow you to design more efficiently, while maintaining your creativity.

The presentation *Don't Design Websites, Design Web SYSTEMS!*,[†] first presented by Todd Nienkerk and Aaron Stanush of Four Kitchens at DrupalCon Copenhagen, illustrates this point perfectly. Working with design agency Thinkso Creative to implement a complex Drupal site for Expeditiary Learning, the Four Kitchens team started with a series of visual designs, site maps and wireframes that Thinkso had put together. All of these provided an excellent design direction for the Four Kitchens team, but because some design elements had been created before Thinkso had chosen Drupal as its platform, several of the elements had to be reconsidered and restructured in order to avoid significant delays or cost impacts in production.

---

† You can get the slide deck at *http://fourkitchens.com/presentations*.

Does this mean that you should know you're designing for Drupal before you start the discovery and user experience phase of a site? Not always. Some projects, particularly ones that involve a high level of user interaction or complexity, can benefit from a platform-agnostic approach in the early phases. What's more important to this process is flexibility: knowing that your designs may have to adapt once you get into technical implementation. This need to adapt is also a key reason that designers should get to know Drupal. By having even a basic understanding of what's happening "under the hood," you can adapt quickly, and avoid the nightmare that eventually befalls every talented web designer: well-meaning implementers who destroy your design to make it fit their framework.

The process for creating an effective Drupal design often depends on the nature of the team and their development strategy. Some Drupal designers focus primarily on aesthetics and layout and give their designs to the developers to implement; other designers prefer to do a little bit of everything, moving from layout to Views configuration to theming as the project progresses, and working with developers to handle the trickier bits of functionality they want to develop.

As you'll probably notice by the time you finish the book, I'm in the latter camp. For me, design for Drupal is about creating a vision, sketching out the possibilities, and moving quickly into prototyping to test the assumptions that I make during the design process. Prototyping early—whether with paper, in a program like Axure or Balsamiq Mockups, or directly in Drupal—helps me make sure that I'm not creating something that will be impossible to implement. It also helps me remain vigilant about all the little things that need to be considered when designing for in a Drupal site, including:

- 404 and 403 pages
- Error messages and content administration links on individual pages
- User profile pages
- Form elements, including the user login block
- The look of block quotes, tables and other things that might be inserted into the content
- Pages for individual content categories, or for social areas of the site

Because we're working in a dynamic framework, any of these pieces might pop up at some point in your user's journey through the site—and it's a safe bet that all of them will. Taking the time to create design that integrates these components with your overall look and feel is part of helping your site look thoughtfully designed and not "Drupally."

The design phase of a Drupal project typically happens in four stages:

Ideation
> During ideation, you're generating ideas for layout, usually in rapid-fire format. Options for ideation include style tiles (sometimes called mood boards), and sketches of wireframes or grid layouts.

Wireframing

Wireframes are basic, component-level mockups of your site's pages. While it's very possible (and increasingly popular) to sketch wireframes with pencil and paper and use those to discuss architecture and content priorities to the client, other options include Adobe Fireworks or Balsamiq Mockups. You can also use a program like Axure RP for wireframing, which allows you to prototype multiple pages within the same document, annotate functionality on the wireframes, and output a functional specification for developers with the click of a button. If you're doing UX work with clients who plan on developing in-house, this can be extraordinarily useful.

Design comps

During layout, you're starting to lay in real content and images, and organize content on the page. Some teams, like San Francisco's Chapter Three, use a hybrid wireframe/design process called "greyboxing" as a way to more rapidly iterate design; others prefer to keep wireframes and design comps as separate components of the design process. See Chapter 5 for more on greyboxing.

Iteration and client signoff

During iteration, wireframes and designs are discussed, debated, and tweaked until the team agrees that it's ready.

Ideally, iteration happens throughout the entire process, with the final result being a set of visual designs that's been agreed on by the team and signed off by the client as "this is what we're going for." Each stage feeds the next; ideation gives you the ideas for wireframes, which inform the designs, etc.

In theory, all of these pieces would happen in turn, and the final designs would be handed over to the implementation team for turning into a Drupal site. In practice, many teams go straight from wireframes into prototyping, and add visual design as a final layer. Others go straight into visual design and then work on implementing those designs in Drupal. As long as you have a solid discovery and information architecture phase to back up your design choices, either approach can work; the important part is having an understanding of what it will take to implement your design choices, and collaborating with your team to make sure that you're designing things that can be implemented.

If you're working solo, it's also vital to know what pieces of the puzzle are beyond the scope of your abilities; having a developer you can call when you need some extra help getting something to work can save you money and headaches down the line.

About the Case Studies

Throughout this book, we'll be focusing on two real-world projects. While this can make it challenging to "follow along at home," for those who like to work that way, I have two reasons for this decision:

1. I'm working on them currently, and I enjoy being able to do two things at once;
2. Focusing on projects like these, as opposed to a single project made up for the book, gives you the chance to see how these ideas work in the real world, with all the frustrations and moments of unexpected joy that happen in real projects.

In Part II, *Design and Layout*, we'll mostly be using my portfolio site, *tzk-design.com*, as an example. This project is currently in the process of being redesigned as I refocus my studio, and it gives me a chance to walk you through the actual process of sketching and creating layouts for a relatively simple site.

The second project, *Urban Homesteaders Unite (UHU)*, is being developed by myself and a colleague, Tricia Okin of Brooklyn, NY's Papercut (*http://papercutny.com*). The site was originally conceived as part of Tricia's MFA thesis (as such, layouts were already created), and I've been working with her to expand upon that original idea and turn it into reality.

The goal of UHU is to connect urban homesteaders, e.g., people into gardening, food preservation, and other city-hippie pursuits, through home-based events, blog posts and connecting with other homesteaders in their neighborhood. This lets me get into deeper areas of Drupal trickiness such as Views relationships and working with user profiles (cue evil laughing).

Through these projects, I can show you a typical Drupal design process—from ideation and sketches to prototyping and applying our look and feel to the site's theme. Let's get started!

CHAPTER 2

The Drupal Designer's Toolkit

While every designer has their own set of applications and supplies that they use for everyday design and prototyping work, certain tools just seem to be particularly useful when working in Drupal. The following is the toolkit that I use for most of my work. Although the last two applications (Coda and Less.app) are Mac-specific, the others are available for Mac or PC.

Balsamiq Mockups

Balsamiq (*http://balsamiq.com/products/mockups*) is a relatively small, but robust, Adobe Air application that helps you create UI mockups incredibly quickly. The program itself contains many of the standard elements you'd expect in a web mockup (text boxes, headlines, video or image comps, etc.), but it's all done in a simple, cartoonish style that helps clients and the design team focus on what's important in the early stages of a project—content organization and hierarchy. Stephanie at Fusion by Top Notch Themes also put together a handy mockup of Drupal-specific components, which you can download here: *http://fusiondrupalthemes.com/story/100325/easier-wireframing -drupal-components-balsamiq-mockups*. I've used it extensively for some of the examples in this book. Figure 2-1 shows the entire set of components.

In the Resources section of this book's website (*http://drupalfordesignersbook.com/re sources*), I've also uploaded a copy of this document (as a .bmml file). For those using the 960 grid system to more efficiently iterate wireframes and design mockups (see Chapter 6 for more info), the master download from 960.gs contains Balsamiq mockup elements for 12, 16, and 24 column layouts.

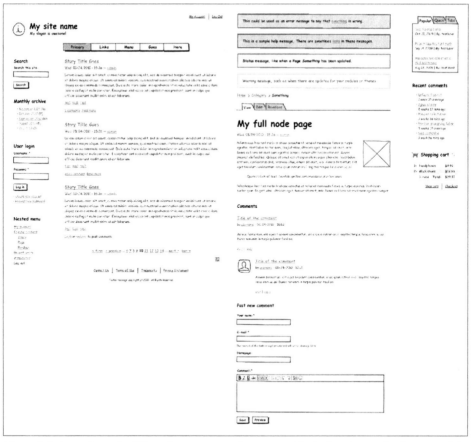

Figure 2-1. A set of standard Drupal components, for your rapid wireframing needs. Courtesy of the fine folks at Fusion by Top Notch themes.

Fireworks

Many designers prefer to use Photoshop or Illustrator for mocking up screen layouts. Although both of these can be very useful (I used Illustrator for years before switching to Fireworks), Fireworks (*http://www.adobe.com/products/fireworks.html*) has both of them beat for a few key reasons:

Share layers among pages

A key component to the magic of Fireworks' multiple pages feature is the ability to share layers (think Photoshop or Illustrator Layers) among several pages in your file. So your header, which is consistent from page to page, can be set up as a single layer, then shared to every page in your document. Change that header once, and every page is changed. Genius! You can also export individual layers as images, which is useful for logos, backgrounds and other elements that you need to transfer from design comp to an image in your theme.

Multiple pages

With Fireworks, you can include multiple pages for the same site in one layout. You can also share layers among different pages. Why is this valuable? Consider this: in most design projects, you might have several pages that you need to lay out for a given design. However, certain elements (such as your grid, or your navigation menu) don't necessarily change from page to page. If you created all of these layouts in Photoshop or Illustrator, and had to make changes to the navigation, you'd have to modify *each one of those files in turn*. With Fireworks, you can change one layer in your file, export it to PDF, and automatically you'd see your changes across all the documents.

PDF Export with clickable goodness

Speaking of multiple pages, you can export your entire document as a multi-page PDF, and use Fireworks' Web Layer to create clickable hot-spots to navigate to other pages, show rollover states, and more. The bonus? All of this can be exported into your PDF—meaning that your client can click around the PDF as if it was a prototype of their website.

Symbols

Symbols are Fireworks' way of collecting elements that are standard in a given document. The beauty of working with symbols is being able to create a symbol, place it, and then quickly edit it when your design changes. Change the symbol, and wherever it appears in your document, the symbols change.

Styles

If you're used to InDesign, you already know what styles are. Styles are standard ways of styling elements in your design, which can be altered and changed at will —and everything you've applied that style to will change along with it. This is especially useful when working with the greyboxing method, which we'll explain in Chapter 5.

Use the same application for wireframing and design

One of the best reasons for using Fireworks over other technologies is that it can be used for everything from wireframes to prototyping to design, all within the same file. You can also export individual layers to images from within Fireworks, which can save a bunch of time in theming, when compared to the usual process of slicing up large layouts in Photoshop or Illustrator. The fact that Fireworks handles vectors (like Illustrator)—but treats them as raster (like Photoshop)—also makes it easier to tweak individual shapes without risking a loss of fidelity.

Much like the set of Drupal components that were created for Balsamiq Mockups (see above), you can also find Fireworks templates for commonly used Drupal elements, courtesy of San Francisco's Chapter Three. In the Resources section of the *Drupal for Designers* site, you'll find both the Chapter Three Fireworks template, and the Greybox template. You can also learn about the Fireworks templates here: *http://www.chapter three.com/blog/nica_lorber/design_drupal_template_approach*. If you prefer to create your own, head over to Chapter 7, where I walk through the process of creating my own Fireworks template for Drupal.

Coda

Coda (*http://panic.com/coda*) is a relatively inexpensive (under $100) application for coding websites. Not only does it allow you to code your pages and upload them in the same screen, it also has the ability to connect to Terminal on your remote server from within the application, which is useful when you're running shell commands, like Drush or Git. Most importantly, Coda's Clips library allows you to keep commonly used code snippets in one place and insert them into your HTML simply by double-clicking. This is extraordinarily useful for theming.

If you're working with a team over the same network, you can also use Bonjour to collaborate with other Coda users in your team. Through the network, you can edit someone else's code (or let them edit yours), save the files, and watch the changes happen in front of you.

LessCSS and Less.app

Less (*http://incident57.com/less*; which you'll read about in Part III, *Prototyping, Theming, and Managing your Markup* of this book) is a CSS framework that allows you to more efficiently create CSS. In addition to allowing you to set variables and "mixins" for colors, fonts, etc. directly in your stylesheets that can be called anywhere else in the stylesheets, it allows you to nest styles within each other. For example, a simple navigation menu might look like this:

```
ul#navigation { list-style: none; display: inline; }
ul#navigation > li { list-style: none; float: left; margin-right: 1em;
    border-right: 1px solid gray; }
ul#navigation > li a { padding: 3px 0; color: black; text-decoration: none;}
ul#navigation > li a:hover { color: white; background: black;
    text-decoration: underline; }
```

In Less, you'd style it thus:

```
ul#navigation {
    list-style: none; display: inline;

    > li {
        list-style: none;
        float: left;
        margin-right: 1em;
        border-right: 1px solid gray;
        padding: 3px 0;

        a {
            padding: 3px 0; color: black;
            text-decoration: none;
```

```
        }

    a:hover {
        color: white; background: black;
        text-decoration: underline;
    }
  }
}
```

When this code is compiled, it will compile into the same code as the first example, but you get to save yourself some typing and keep all your code for a given element organized in one place. This is especially useful when working in Drupal, as you'll often find yourself customizing a much larger amount of CSS for any given area of a site—from a particular page, to a block, to the entire sidebar. You'll read more about the awesomeness that is Less CSS in Chapter 15.

Ordinarily, you would compile your Less code using a small Javascript file either on your site's server, or directly in your template files. While this is one way of doing it, it forces a load on the server that you may not want, and it could mess you up if your user is in a browser that doesn't have Javascript enabled. Yes, it does happen sometimes. This is where Less.app comes in. It's a tiny Mac application that sits open while you work, and "watches" any folder that you put into it for changes to .less files. As you're working, every time you save the file, Less.app will compile your Less code for you into a .css file, allowing you to more efficiently see what you're doing. Figure 2-2 is a screenshot of the app, which is available at *http://incident57.com/less*.

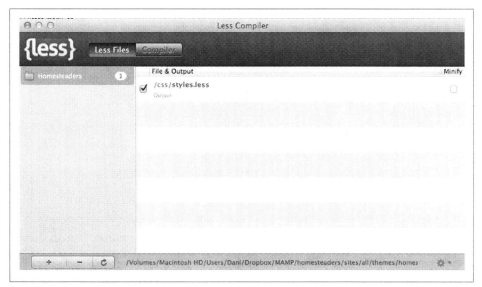

Figure 2-2. The handy Less.app "watches" any folder that you drag into it and compiles your LessCSS into CSS as you work

PART II

Design and Layout

CHAPTER 3

Sketch Many, Show One

Like many designers, when doing a logo design for a client, I'll often sketch many different options, and then refine the 3–4 most effective options to show the client. This works because the client feels that they have a choice among several good options, but they aren't overwhelmed with decisions. It also works because they know I've carefully vetted each option, and decided that any of them can work equally well.

Given this approach to branding work, it would make sense that we would want to give the client a few different options for their website's layout or information architecture, and work with the client to choose the best option. In my experience, this approach fails for some very important reasons:

- **It keeps conversation focused on visuals, not content or organization of information**. I cannot emphasize this enough: the early stages of creating a website should be focused on content and communication priorities, *not on visual ones*. While visual communication is also an important part of the web design process, those conversations are best had after you've already established your content hierarchies, and seen how real content flows through your site.

- **There's a lot more to decide in a web layout than there is in a logo design**. A logo, while essential to an effective brand, is a relatively small part of the overall identity of an organization. As such, the decision of which logo to choose is often a relatively quick one, and the client's focus is exclusively on this one image. With a web layout, there are many more variables to pay attention to. Does the navigation make sense? Have we covered everything that should (and shouldn't) be on this page? Throwing aesthetic decisions into the mix too early in the game prevents stakeholders from focusing on these other questions, which can hinder the user experience of the site.

Because of these concerns, I recommend a "sketch many, show one" approach to wireframes and design comps. With this approach, you sketch a bunch of different options for a web layout—usually the home page and at least one interior page—and pick the one that works best according to the project's goals to refine and present to the client.

This approach can be very successful, especially for clients who tend to focus on too many things at once. However, there's a caveat: whenever you present work in this fashion, it's important to reassure the client that you're showing them one approach based on what your research suggests will work best, and that this approach is open to change based on the client's objectives and preferences. Also, although clients have rarely needed it, I also leave room in my contracts for a complete shift in direction, if the client feels strongly that the solution we've come up with doesn't fit their needs.

Although some designers bristle at the idea of only showing one layout option, I've found that this approach works well for a number of reasons:

- It keeps the conversation focused (which becomes more important as projects gain complexity)
- It moves you and the client through the process more efficiently, so you can move into prototyping more quickly
- It shows confidence in your approach, which can give the client confidence in your team

Perhaps most importantly, by presenting one design that can be iterated upon, you're making it easier on stakeholders and the production team by focusing your efforts in one direction, rather than trying two or three directions to see which one fits. Additionally, if your process includes a solid IA and UX phase prior to the visual design phase (which it should), showing one layout tells the client that you've had a lot of time to get to know their brand.

Ideation: Methods and Madness

A growing number of designers, including Milwaukee-based Mike Rohde (interviewed below) have started showing their early sketches to clients, as a way to present truly low-fi wireframes and keep the discussion focused on user experience and not visual design. In practice, I've found that the success of this approach often depends on the client and the rest of the project team. With some clients and developers, I toss out a quick sketch in my journal, show it to them, and they get it completely. With others, unless it's mocked up in a pixel-perfect Fireworks or Photoshop document, you spend more time defending your choice to sketch on paper than you do discussing potential design approaches.

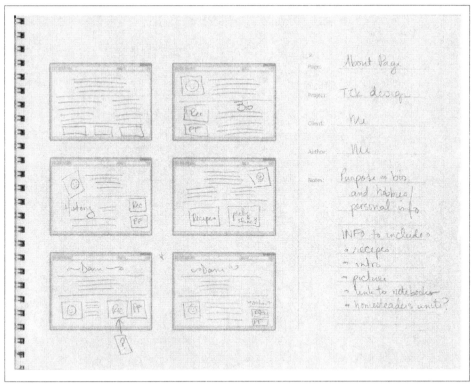

Figure 3-1. This six-screen sketch sheet, available from Adaptive Path's website, makes it easy to sketch multiple ideas for a page before refining the most effective concept

Whether you build out your wireframes in software or keep them strictly paper-based, the point of sketches is to come up with as many ideas as possible, get rid of the ones that don't work, and pare it all down to the one or two best ideas you generated, and then talk those through with your stakeholders. Lately, I've been starting my sketches with the six-up templates from UX firm Adaptive Path (*http://www.adaptivepath.com/ideas/sketchboards-discover-better-faster-ux-solutions*; also see Figure 3-1) to help force myself to come up with more than one or two options for a given page. Having to create six small sketches at a time helps move you past the obvious choices, and often, I'll find that one of my later options works even better than my first instinct.

Once I've worked out a couple of ideas on the six-up template (or just created a bunch of thumbnails in my journal), I'll choose the one that seems to work best and work it into a larger sketch, either using a sheet from the Browser Sketch Pad from *uistencils.com*, or mocking up a quick wireframe in Balsamiq Mockups (see Figure 3-2).

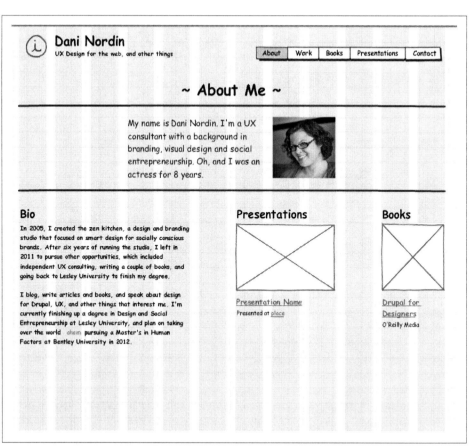

Figure 3-2. Using Balsamiq Mockups to refine one of the earlier pencil sketches. This mockup is based on a 12-column, 960-pixel grid, ala 960.gs

From the Trenches: Mike Rohde, UI Designer and Illustrator

Mike Rohde is a UX/UI Designer from Milwaukee who is known, among other things, as the illustrator for 37Signals' book "Rework." As a designer who works on a variety of complex interaction challenges ranging from websites to multi-platform applications, Mike uses pencil sketches extensively in his creative process, and considers them an essential component of client communication.

Dani: When you do interface work, you show your clients hand-drawn sketches. How do you find that that has served you as you do UX work, whether it's Drupal or any other platform?

Mike: I've found that sketches work really well for helping to make a quick transition from idea to a concept that the client can really get their head around. There's a level where you can [verbally] say "yes, well it'll do this, and we can make it do that," and if they're not a web developer or even a designer, they often can't picture what that thing will look like when you describe it. In fact, it might become more confusing to them as they're trying to envision it. The other danger is that you describe it and they have one idea, then when you show it to them, it's actually a different idea than what they had envisioned.

The challenge when you go straight to a finished project—let's say you invest a lot of time and energy creating a prototype—and you haven't gotten very good information, or the client hasn't been as forthcoming as you'd like—you may have invested a lot of time and energy in creating a prototype that isn't going to work for the client, and you'll have to start over. Hand-drawn sketches provide something in between. You can do it to many different degrees; I've done everything from incredibly loose sketches that I've shown along with a little description and received approval on to very detailed wire-frame-type sketches.

It varies depending on the client and what I wanted to show, but it's been very effective. One of the main things I've noticed about sketches is that clients aren't so afraid of them. One of the things that happens with wireframes, mockups or prototypes—or anything that feels like it's at some level of "finished"—is that clients will sometimes feel that there's too much progress and they're afraid to say something. They won't say so directly, but they might feel like "I can't really criticize it because they've already spent so much time on it." But that lack of up-front feedback ends up coming out in the end, and at the back end of the project we end up noticing things, and needing more changes, which are more expensive to implement. By giving them a sketch, you can head them off on some issues and let them feel like they can have some input because, you know, it's just a pencil sketch. I can criticize that—they'll just do another one right?

Dani: When you look at a wireframe that's been done in Fireworks, it's often easy for the client to critique like, "oh, is that really going to be the font?" I imagine that, with sketches, there's a lot less of that. You're really focused on "this is the hierarchy of information on this screen"—which is really what you want to be talking about in the wireframe stage.

Mike: I think it comes down to setting expectations. Many times when I do sketch work, I'll work with Basecamp, and upload a scan of a sketch that I've done, with a pretty detailed description of what they can expect to happen and what my thoughts are. If it's a combination of notes and a sketch itself, I'll very often include notes like "this will do that" with an arrow pointing to a button that will do such and such or so and so. But then I'll provide a description. And then when I speak to the client, I'll talk to them on the phone and point to parts of the sketch, and we can even go in and mark the sketch up during an in-person meeting (See Figures 3-3, 3-4, and 3-5).

What that does is bring them into the process of decision making and understanding. I think that if I prepare them and say, "look, this is a very high-level sketch of the broad idea that we're going for—we're not going to show fonts or colors or any of those things," then it seems to work pretty well. Again, I think it's a question of setting expectations that happens with every kind of design that we do. Whether it's sketches or mockups, and then explaining your process.

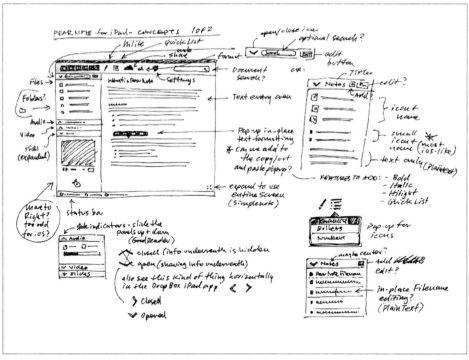

Figure 3-3. An early sketch concept wireframe for Pear Note on the iPad. Image credit: Mike Rohde, rohdesign.com/usefulfruit.com

Once I've mocked up my wireframe, I'll use what I've mocked up to validate the concepts about content priorities, navigation, etc., that we established in the information architecture/UX phase with the client and design team. For personal projects, or projects where there's a piece of the interaction that I am still trying to understand, I may also go straight into a prototype, either in a program like Axure or in Drupal, so I can make sure what I'm thinking of is feasible and show clients the real interaction we're trying to create. Prototyping, whether I'm doing it myself or with a developer's help, also helps me work out areas of the content that may require special treatment, like videos or content that needs to be formatted a certain way. I'll also use this opportunity to start collecting images, type treatments, and color options in a series of style tiles, which I'll start showing to the client after we've established the information priorities. We'll talk about style tiles in the next chapter.

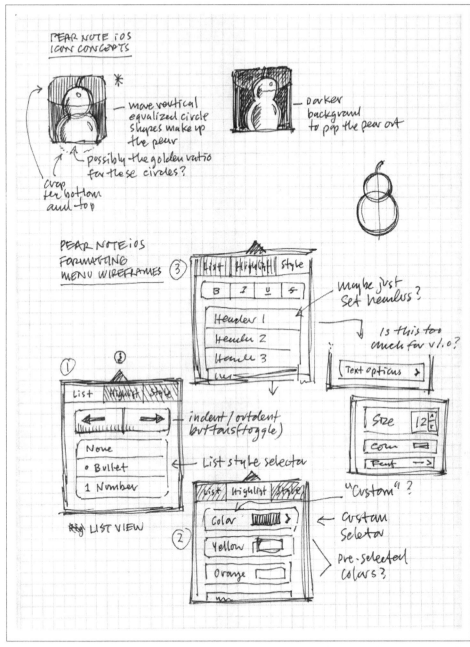

Figure 3-4. Rough concept sketches for the Pear Note iPad icon and menus. These were created to explore some ideas with Chad (iPad developer) before jumping back to Photoshop for mockups. I explored all kinds of ideas and shared them with Chad. We discussed further and then I created final mockups which Chad used for reference in the final development of the app. Image credit: Mike Rohde, rohdesign.com/usefulfruit.com

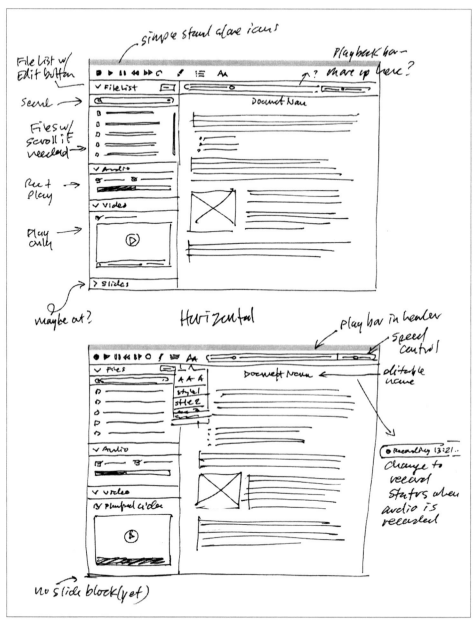

Figure 3-5. Here are two detailed wireframe-like concept sketches, used to explore ideas for working out the Pear Note for iPad interface details. In the end the app was simplified a bit from these sketches, focusing on core features for v1 (audio and text). Image credit: Mike Rohde, rohdesign.com/usefulfruit.com

CHAPTER 4

Using Style Tiles to Explore Design Ideas

A style tile (sometimes called a *mood board*) is a simple collection of images, fonts, colors and other inspiration to inform your design. The important difference between a sketch or layout concept and a style tile is its lack of structure; while a layout comp is meant to represent an entire page, a style tile is best kept simple. In a style tile, you collect elements that make sense for the project, shuffle them around, and see how they work. Style tiles are also meant to be works in progress; while the hope is that layout comps will only reach the client when they're in good enough condition to be close to final, a series of style tiles can be shown to a client at early stages of the project, to gauge aesthetic preferences and make sure you're on the same wavelength. They're also great for fleshing out ideas, or keeping track of visual stories for future projects. Figures 4-1 and 4-2 are style tiles for the redesign of my studio website, currently in progress.

As you can see, this isn't a complete layout as much as a visual exploration of fonts, colors, and treatments for different areas of the site. When it comes down to theming the site, I might end up doing something entirely different—but at the very least, I'm developing a sense of the mood that I'm trying to create, and working out how the different types of images I will need to show will be displayed, how headlines should be treated, etc.

Style tiles can be created at any stage of a project. They're especially good for exploring ideas early on, while you're wireframing, as a way to collect your thoughts about visual solutions before you are ready to explore them with the client. The most important thing to note about them, particularly if you plan on discussing them with clients, is that *style tiles should not look like a web page*. Their purpose is to explore visual elements and treatments, not to create a layout for the website.

Figure 4-1. An initial style tile for tzk-design.com

Figure 4-2. A second style tile, with a different feel to it. After considering the two, I decided to build on the approach in this one, which I refine in Chapter 7

The benefit of showing style tiles instead of design layouts is similar to the benefit of starting a discussion with sketches instead of a more formalized wireframe:

It's fast
> A set of style tiles can take as little as 1–3 hours to put together, often even less. They're also much easier and more efficient to iterate than full design comps; rather than fleshing out these ideas in full designs that then have to be iterated again and again, you can use style tiles to quickly identify a set of visual guidelines that will guide the overall look and feel of a site quickly and cheaply. In fact, I've sometimes ended up doing style tiles while doing research or information architecture for a client project, throwing ideas into a Fireworks file as ideas come up.

It's modular
> Because you're using the style tiles to explore visual approaches rather than to set up a specific set of layouts for a given section of the site, style tiles fit in very well with the modularity of the Drupal design process. In some cases, you can even start theming based on style tiles instead of having to do full layout comps.

It brings the client into the conversation
> This increases their confidence in your approach, and lets them see the design process happening in front of them. Having the client involved in the conversation at an early stage in the process helps them feel like they have "ownership" of the design, which increases the likelihood that they'll approve the proposed design when you're ready to finalize the look and feel of the site.

It helps keep the conversation focused
> By walking the client through a set of style tiles, rather than a complete layout, you can keep the conversation focused on aesthetics, rather than content and placement—which, ideally, will have already been settled by the time you've started discussing the style tiles. This helps keep everyone focused on the visuals at the time when you're actually supposed to be focused on the visuals.

What you're doing, in essence, is setting up a series of stylistic conventions to be used across the site's various elements. This can help you save time by letting you go straight from wireframe to implementation, using the style tiles to guide the theming process, rather than creating design layouts that dictate the design of a specific page, but can't necessarily be carried over to the other pages.

Once you've iterated your style tiles to the point where you and the client agree that you've found the best visual approach, you have a choice in how to proceed. If you've already started getting some content into a development site (which you ideally will by this point), you can start applying these standards across your site's theme, and give clients the chance to see how these visuals will play out with real content. If you're still working out issues with specific types of content, or special areas of the site, you may want to start working the style tiles into full design comps, preferably with examples of real content from the client's site.

Whether you go to theming straight from your style tiles or you go from style tiles to full design comps, it's important to consider not just the basics, like headers, paragraphs, and sidebar boxes, but to think holistically about the types of content and functionality that you're going to be building. In Chapter 5, *Design Layout: Covering All Your Bases*, we'll look at some of the elements that should be considered when designing for a Drupal implementation.

Design Layout: Covering All Your Bases

Once you've established a visual direction with style tiles and you're ready to get into design comps (or start theming), you want to make sure you're considering all of the elements you may end up dealing with in the process of creating a Drupal site. For example, how do you want to treat block quotes? Tables of data? What about pagers for list pages? The following is a brief list of the elements you should consider when creating your style tiles, adapted from San Francisco Drupal firm Chapter Three's excellent blog post, *Design for Drupal—a Template Approach*:[*]

- Header text and links
- Footer text and links
- H1 - H5 tags
- Body
- Link
- Unordered List
- Blockquote
- Image Styles
- Code snippets in text
- Admin Tabs (the View/Edit/etc. tabs listed on pages for logged-in users)
- Secondary Admin Tabs (the links listed under admin tabs)
- Collapsible Field Sets and Accordions
- Headers and typography for blocks
- "More" button
- "Read More" link/button
- Form elements and labels
- Tags

[*] *http://www.chapterthree.com/blog/nica_lorber/design_drupal_template_approach*

- Pagination for Views listings
- Tables
- Error Messages
- Status Messages
- Warning Messages
- Help Messages
- Blog post titles
- Author and post date information
- Breadcrumbs

While you don't have to style every last element within a style tile, it's useful to keep them in the back of your mind while playing around with ideas. In fact, you may even consider doing two style tiles for a given project: one for front-facing pages (i.e., what the user sees) and another for client-facing (i.e., site editors, etc.) pages.

Once you've gone over the style tiles with your client, and you're confident that the visual approach you've decided on will work for them, it's time to start looking at the layout of your pages. As with the mood board elements mentioned above, the key here is to make sure you've got your bases covered. While it's not necessary to try to create a design comp for every single page in your Drupal implementation, there are certain pages that will show up over and over again in your layouts, and it's useful to set a visual standard for each of these types of pages. When creating your design layouts, be sure to consider the following types of pages:

- Single node page, with one sidebar
- Single node page, with two sidebars
- Single node page, with no sidebars
- Blog listing, with pagination
- Single blog page, with comments
- User profile pages
- Category pages
- Groups pages (if applicable)
- 404 and 403 pages
- Contact forms
- And finally, the home page

If you're working in Fireworks (see Chapter 2 for the various reasons why you should be), the good news is that you can collect all of these pages into one document, use Hotspots to create links among the various pages, and export the whole thing as a multi-page PDF that your client can then click around to see the flow of their website.

If you want to get a head start on your design layouts, Chapter Three has created a multi-page Fireworks file you can download to get started. The file, available at *http://www.chapterthree.com/blog/nica_lorber/design_drupal_template_approach*, has the following pages already created:

- News/Blog page
- News/Blog page with sidebar
- Basic Node Page + Typography
- Basic Node Page w/sidebar
- News/Blog Views
- Admin Login w/tabs
- Admin: Collapsible Boxes
- Admin: Table
- Contact Us
- Profile Page
- Error Message

While a couple of the pages (such as the admin areas) aren't something you typically need to worry about with Drupal 7 theming, they're extremely useful for Drupal 6 projects, where the admin theme is often the same as the site's theme. You also want to make sure that you consider things like admin links on individual pages, the site's log in page, and profile pages, which don't use the Drupal admin theme. In a couple of chapters, I'll walk you through the process of creating your own Fireworks template, using the example of the new version of *tzk-design.com*, currently in development.

Greyboxing: An In-Between Option

While it's often tempting to go straight from wireframes to design layouts, in some cases an interaction that you're trying to create is complex enough that it makes sense to take a step in between. Other times, you might find yourself dealing with a very tight deadline for a project, and you need to move from wireframe to design more quickly than you would normally—but you still want to make sure that the client's attention stays focused on content and information priorities before you jump straight into colors and fonts.

One alternative to going straight from wireframes to design is greyboxing, a process outlined by Chapter Three's Floor Van Herreweghe in her blog post "Designing in the Grey" (*http://www.chapterthree.com/greyboxing*) and a recent presentation at Drupal Design Camp in Boston (*http://boston2011.design4drupal.org/sessions/art-wireframing-using-greybox-model-visualize-user-experience*). Greyboxing is, in essence, a middle step between wireframes (simple layouts with placeholders/blank boxes for content) and design layouts (which are often meant to represent the ultimate design of the site's pages). It gives you an opportunity to design while you're wireframing, but it also gives you the opportunity to move from wireframe to design sooner than you would in a traditional wireframe-to-layout design process, which is useful for projects that require a very strict timeline.

The idea is that you already have a sense—through your sketches—of what the content for the page is going to be, and you've already got an idea of some different visual approaches for the page, which you incorporated into your style tiles. But you're not quite ready to fully take the leap into full-on design mode—for example, if there are content issues the client still needs to settle on. The important thing to note here is that *greyboxing does not replace sketching*; rather, it gives you an interim step in the process before you get to a complete design. For example, Figure 5-1 is an example of a page layout for our Urban Homesteaders Unite site, created using the greyboxing technique.

In projects with very tight deadlines, greyboxing can also be a way to go from sketches into a starting point for your layout while maintaining the client's attention on content organization and flow rather than color preferences. In her session at Design for Drupal Camp, Van Herreweghe used an example from a project that only allowed three weeks for the entire design phase; going into greyboxing quickly allowed her to quickly set a visual standard, and then evolve the visual standard with colors, fonts, etc. as the layout gets closer to what it should be. This is another benefit to using Fireworks for this process; Fireworks allows you to set up Styles (similar to InDesign's Styles palette), which you can simply edit to change all instances of a given element within your document. This means that you can start with your greybox layout, then change the styles to create the final design.

Another thing that can help you make your layout decisions more efficiently is working with a grid framework; in the next chapter, we'll discuss 960.gs, one of my favorites.

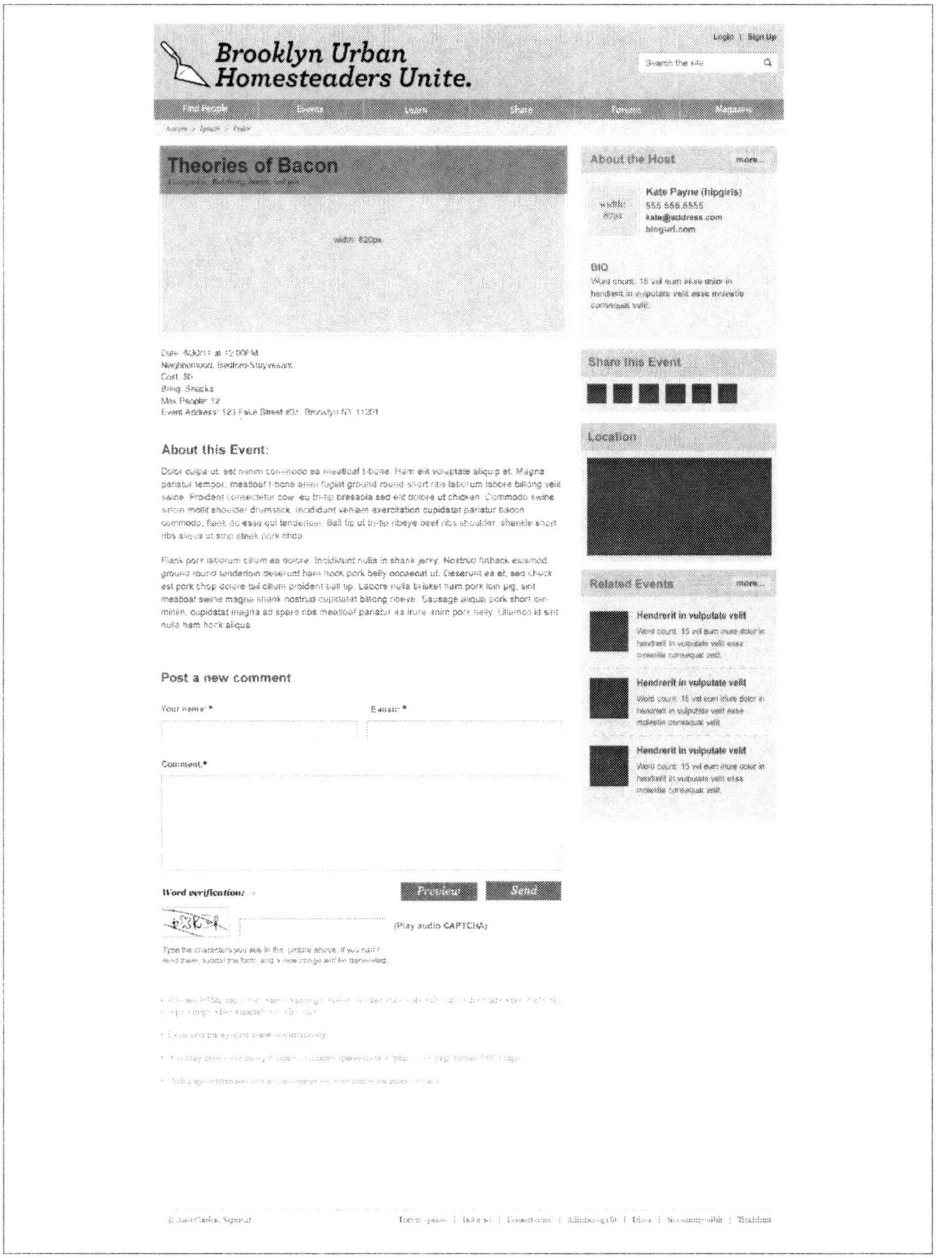

Figure 5-1. This Event page has been laid out using the greyboxing technique. Note that some visual standards have already started to be set, images have placeholders connected to them, but everything is still in varying shades of grey

CHAPTER 6

Working with Layout Grids

> We can think of grids, therefore, as a springboard for creativity. They lay a foundation through which a designer can create solutions to problems large and small, and in doing so help readers, users, and audiences find that which all humans seek: a sense of order within disorder.[*]

As you may have noticed from the series of semi-transparent rectangles overlaying a few of the examples in this book, I use grid systems fairly often in my work. There are several different grid systems available for websites, many created for specific projects by developers who decided to give their work back to the design community. This chapter will focus on the one I've been using for years, 960.gs. 960 is certainly not the only option for a grid system; however, it is one that has received a lot of attention and support in the Drupal community. The 960 grid system (960.gs), developed by Nathan Smith, is incorporated into both the NineSixty (*drupal.org/project/ninesixty*) and Omega (*drupal.org/project/omega*) Drupal themes, and the 960 grid generator (*grids.heroku.com/*) allows you to create your own version of the 960 grid by setting a column number, width, and gutter width (Figure 6-1).

Why Use a Grid?

Grids have been a standard part of the practice of graphic design for decades. In addition to providing much-needed structure in a layout, grids also serve to make information easier for us to process. When confronted with any layout—whether it's a printed brochure or a website—our eyes struggle first to instill some sort of order to what we're seeing. When we're confronted with a chaotic layout, particularly when an element in that layout is just slightly misaligned with an element near it, we focus more on the misalignment than the message or content of the piece. Grids, then, give us the ability to create that order, and to make it easier for the people accessing our content to pay attention to what's important about the page. See Figure 6-2 for an example.

---

[*] Vinh, Khoi. *Ordering Disorder: Grid Systems in Web Design*, p. 13

Figure 6-1. Nathan Smith's lovely 960.gs is a good starting place for working with grids in your web design. If you want to try your hand at a custom grid, he even includes a custom CSS generator

Additionally, and particularly in regards to layout for the web, having a grid system helps create a set of known constraints that can help you focus your design solutions. As the logistics of implementing our solutions for the web continue to grow more complex, the structure provided by different grid systems gives you one less thing to worry about when implementing your layout.

This means that you can iterate on a design more quickly. Rather than thinking of elements on a page in terms of pixel widths, which can range from 100px to 960px or more, a grid system allows you to think of things in terms of how many columns it takes up. This is remarkably useful in terms of efficiency; instead of kvetching about whether a sidebar should be 200px or 234px wide, for example, and spending your time worried about padding and floating, etc.—you can tweak things simply by changing the sidebar's class from 2 columns to 3 columns wide.

Figure 6-2. Elements that are just slightly misaligned can create distraction for users

Grids in Wireframing

Working with a grid system also makes wireframing more efficient. I find that a well-constructed grid even facilitates sketching ideas; having a grid right there on the page makes it easier to consider issues of hierarchy, proportion and overall layout without second-guessing yourself. The classic 960 grid uses 12 or 16 columns; however, a 24 column grid was recently added, which has been built into the Omega theme. Personally, I prefer the 24-column layout (see Figure 6-4); it has enough columns to be very flexible (for example, you can have either three or four columns of content in a given region), but not so many that it's hard to figure out how many to use for a given element. Figure 6-3, a very early wireframe for my personal site, uses a 12-column grid. In Figure 6-4, I've revised the wireframe to use a 24-column grid.

Grids in Theming

There are several base themes available for Drupal that have the 960.gs grid built right into them. You will learn more about two of them, NineSixty (*drupal.org/project/ninesixty*) and Omega (*drupal.org/project/omega*) in Chapter 10, *Working with Base Themes*; however, several base themes are available that incorporate 960.gs in their styles. Two other options available for Drupal 7 are:

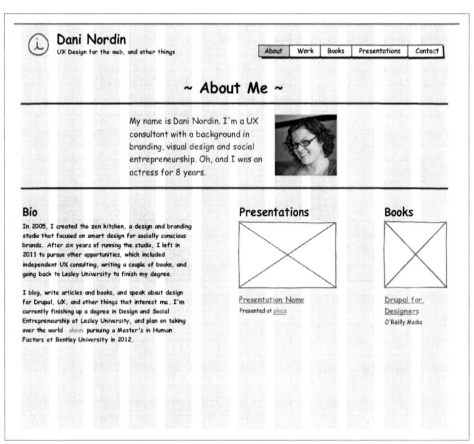

Figure 6-3. This quick wireframe for the "About" page of my website refresh uses a 12-column grid

Panels 960gs *(drupal.org/project/panels_960gs)*

> This is an HTML5-based theme that incorporates the 960 grid system with Panels (*drupal.org/project/panels*), a module that allows you to create customized drag-and-drop layouts for multiple purposes. Panels is a module created by the Earl Miles, the creator of Views. I can't say I've ever used this theme, as I don't tend to use Panels in my sites; however, for those who use Panels regularly, it seems like a great option.

Sky *(drupal.org/project/sky)*

> Developed by Jacine Luisi of Gravitek Labs, Sky isn't so much a base theme as it is a nice, basic theme with sensible defaults. It's also Color module enabled, which means that you can easily change the default color scheme of the theme in your site's Appearance settings. I used this theme for a project I worked on in early 2011; while many of the defaults seemed very sensible, I found there were a large number of overrides needed in order to customize it to the level I needed for the project.

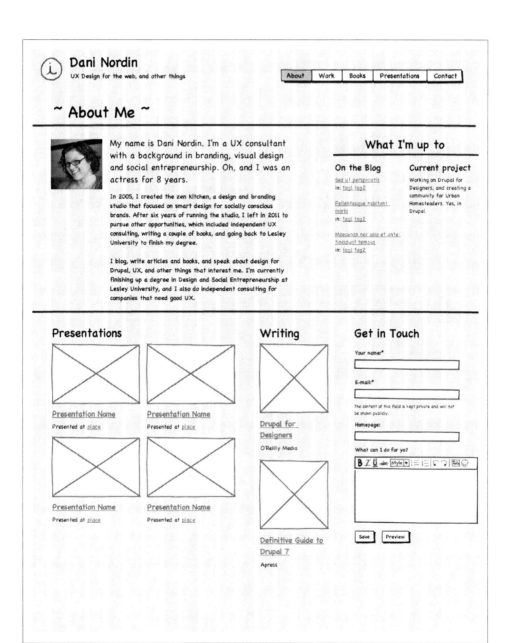

Figure 6-4. Switching to a 24-column grid gives me a bit more flexibility; I can fit a bit more on the page, but still keep things organized

Aside from the ones listed, just about any base theme can be adjusted to incorporate the 960 grid system. Simply download the appropriate grid from 960.gs (either the standard grid, or a custom grid of your own wicked devising, using the custom grid generator), load the CSS files into your subtheme, and add their names to your sub-theme's *.info* file. Then, sketch your layout using the grid, and incorporate those grid values into your subtheme's template files, or use the Block Class module to add a custom grid value (represented as a class, like "grid-2") to a block in your theme. See Chapter 14 for a description of the Block Class module.

Anatomy of a Grid Layout

960 (and many other grid systems) work like this: you start with your *container* width. The *container* is just that; it contains your grid columns. Regardless of the number of columns (12, 16, or 24), in each container div, you'll have a series of <divs> inside the containers, each of which has a certain column width, denoted by the class `grid-`*[number]*. So, for example, let's say I have a layout like Figure 6-5, with a 12-column grid, a content area of 6 columns and 2 sidebars of 3 columns each.

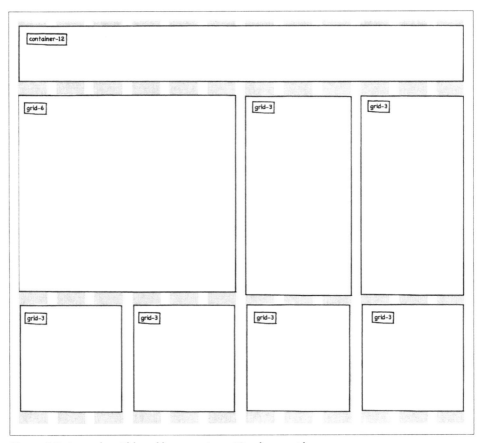

Figure 6-5. A sample grid-based layout, using a 12-column grid

If I was building that out in code, it might look like this:

```
<div id="page" class="container-12">
    <div id="header" class="container-12">
    </div>
    <div id="middle" class="container-12">
        <div id="content" class="grid-6 alpha">
                    <p>Some text goes here</p>
        </div>
        <div id="sidebar-first" class="grid-3">
                    <p>some text goes here</p>
        </div>
         <div id="sidebar-second" class="grid-3">
                    <p>some text goes here</p>
        </div>
    </div>
    <div id="footer" class="container-12">
                    Etc. Etc. Etc.
    </div>
</div>
```

As you can see, each of the horizontal sections of our layout—header, middle and footer—is given a `container` class, while each vertical section in our layout gets a `grid` class with a number corresponding to the number of columns we want the section to have.

In addition to the grid values, 960.gs also has `push` and `pull` classes that will apply negative or positive margins to a given layout in order to give you a content-first layout (helping search engines and screen readers better deal with your site's content) while maintaining the aesthetic we want. For example, let's say that we want that first sidebar to show up on the left side of the page instead of after the content area, but we still want to keep the sidebar's content showing up after the content area in our markup. In our "middle" section, we could adjust our markup thus:

```
<div id="middle" class="container-12">
    <div id="content" class="grid-6 push-3">
            <p>Some text goes here</p>
    </div>
    <div id="sidebar-first" class="grid-3 pull-3">
            <p>some text goes here</p>
    </div>
    <div id="sidebar-second" class="grid-3">
            <p>some text goes here</p>
    </div>
</div>
```

There's also a `prefix` and `suffix` class for adding space between elements; for example, if you wanted to put some air in between the content area and the second sidebar, you could change the markup like this:

```
<div id="middle" class="container-12">
    <div id="content" class="grid-6 push-3 suffix-1">
        <p>Some text goes here</p>
    </div>
```

```
    <div id="sidebar-first" class="grid-3 pull-6">
        <p>some text goes here</p>
    </div>
    <div id="sidebar-second" class="grid-2">
        <p>some text goes here</p>
    </div>
</div>
```

It may sound a bit complicated, but as long as all the numbers in your grid add up to the width of your container, you're all set. Here's a quick checklist for doing the math:

- *Push* and *pull* values should match the widths of the elements with which they're being swapped. If our content area above (`grid-6`) needs to swap places with our first sidebar (`grid-3`), the sidebar should have a class of `pull-6`, and our content area should have a class of `push-3`.

- `Prefix` and `suffix` values add to your column total. So if you have a 12-column grid, and your content area has a width of `grid-5` and a suffix of `suffix-1`, you have exactly 6 columns left in your grid. This is especially noticeable when wireframing, and it's also one of the reasons I like 24-column grids.

From the Trenches: Todd Nienkerk, Four Kitchens

Four Kitchens is a Drupal shop in Austin, TX, that specializes in helping clients create large-scale websites. They also run DrupalCamp Austin, a yearly Drupal event, and they co-created and co-maintain Pressflow, a specialized Drupal distribution optimized for large-scale implementations. Todd is a vocal advocate of 960.gs, and gives presentations on the system at Drupal events around the country.

Dani: Why do you love grids?

Todd: My own reason is the one that I perhaps don't hype enough in the talks I give about grid design, but it's a constraint that frees me. Just as a painter would first choose a palette, or limit the size of the canvas—you impose a limit on what you design, because then you can innovate within those constraints.

If you have not only a blank canvas, but a blank canvas of any size, or shape, or orientation, how do you even start, really? Whatever you're creating, you have to make that first decision. A grid is like that first decision. What's even better about it is that it's a first decision that's kind of already made for you; you don't have to feel like, "Oh, did I screw up?" You're rarely going to say, "I picked a width of 920 pixels for my website. I hope I don't regret this in a year."

Typesetting is a really good analogy for this kind of thing, because it's why grids were developed back in the day. You had to create grids to set your type, because you couldn't build actual typesetting machines for each book. You had to develop something that you could reuse from one book to another.

Using a grid allows you to say, "my content is going to be somewhere in this range," and now I have fewer decisions to make. Consider the paradox of choice; if you have too much choice, you're going to freeze up and maybe not make any decision whatsoever. But if you have a limited number of choices—for example, 12 columns to work

---

with—you can configure them in a finite way, and it's easier to make decisions about that configuration. You can have 12 1-column spaces, you can have 1 12-column space, you can have 3 4-column spaces, etc. It's actually freeing, because it limits your choices, and you can propel the process forward. You get beyond that first stage of existential, "what am I going to do with this giant blank canvas of infinity?" and create a starting point from which you can move forward.

Dani: Knowing that I have a certain amount of structure helps me come up with ideas more quickly, because I know the language of the grid. I frequently do wireframes where I specify "grid-5," "grid-7," etc. One of the things I love about 960 is that, if a column suddenly appears way too wide, you could just move down a number on the grid class, and it's done. Boom. Resized. There's none of this thing you have to do with Zen, where you have to change values in four different stylesheets.

Todd: Yes, the ease of use of a grid system—and I don't think this is exclusive to 960, but I think that 960 does it best in terms of setting the tone for this kind of thing—is that changing stuff, and visualizing the markup and CSS is orders of magnitude simpler. It's no longer about "is this 127 pixels?" or "what's my negative margin here?" It's a shortcut, or shorthand; if I'm working in a 16-column grid, I know that a single column is 40 pixels wide, and it has a margin-right and margin-left of 10 pixels. I know that academically. But when I'm in the zone, and I just need to move things around, and I need to rapidly iterate and prototype, I don't want to be thinking about, "why did my layout break? Why did this object flow to the next row?"

With the grid, I can simply look at the numbers and say, "all of these numbers add up to 12; I'm done." If I decide one thing is too wide, and I want to make it 1 column shorter, I just have to add a column somewhere else and I'm done. Thinking of widths in terms of columns, rather than pixels, is a huge time-saver. How often have we had to do a web design with a calculator app open? Why not create the math up front, and never have to think about it again?

But What About All These Presentational Classes? There Must Be a Better Way!

While 960.gs offers a ton of flexibility, and can make constructing a page more efficient, it must be acknowledge that it adds a fair amount of code to your site—not only the CSS files that construct the grid, but also the presentational classes needed to set up page defaults (`grid-x`, `push-x`, etc.). For those who pride themselves on fully semantic code (organized by hierarchy, presentation well separated from content, etc.), this can be a major annoyance. What if there was another option—an option that could set up a grid for you without all those annoying extra CSS classes?

Currently, there is one option: Susy (*susy.oddbird.net/*). Susy is billed as a way to make "unobtrusive grids for designers." Susy allows you to create custom grids using Compass and Sass (command-line CSS tools; see *http://compass-style.org/*), without any presentational classes showing up in your markup. While Susy looks very powerful, there are some caveats to its awesomeness:

- **It requires knowledge of the command line**. You'll need to install a Ruby gem in order to install the Susy plugin, and you'll also need the command line to start a new project and to compile your CSS once you've set your definitions.

- **It requires knowledge of Compass and Sass**. Compass and Sass are, as mentioned earlier, command-line CSS tools. They are similar to LessCSS, which you will read about later in this book, but instead of using Javascript to compile your CSS, they do everything through the command line.

- **You need to do math. Lots of math**. In order to plan out and define your grid, you'll need to do some advanced planning and set up the math for your grid.

I'm not saying that any of these things are deal-breakers; over the years, I've actually gotten somewhat cozy with the command line, and I was one of those obnoxious kids who did math for fun. However, the power of Compass, Sass, and Susy come with pretty steep learning curves; every designer will have their own take as to how much of that learning curve they're willing (or have time) to take on. For those who are interested in using Compass, but aren't ready for the command line just yet, there is a reasonably priced ($7) app available for both Mac and Windows that will compile your Compass for you. I don't know if it also works with Susy, but it's worth a try.

The New CSS Grid Layout module: The Future Is Now

With all this talk of grid systems for the web, the future looks promising. An actual CSS Grid Layout module is, as of this writing, in editor's draft at the w3c (*http://dev .w3.org/csswg/css3-grid-align/*). The CSS Grid Layout module will allow you to define a basic grid in the top of your CSS, and position your elements directly within the grid.

For example, let's go back to Figure 6-5 and see how we'd construct that grid with this new module.

The first thing we'd want to do is define our grid container. We'll call that #page in our CSS. Since most of our widths are actually grid-3 (in 960.gs terms), we can probably get away with doing 4 columns instead of 12. We'll also need three rows: one for the header, one for the middle, and one for the bottom:

```
#page {
    display: grid;
    grid-columns: 1fr 1fr 1fr 1fr;
    grid-rows: 130px auto auto;
}
```

The "fr" in the grid-columns is shorthand for "fractions;" it's a percentage of the overall grid.

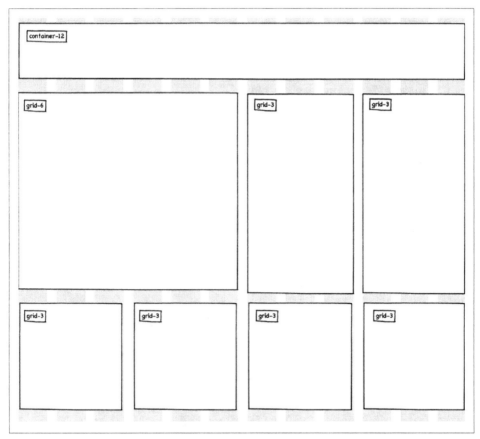

Figure 6-6. Revisiting our 12-column layout from earlier

This will set up our grid with four equal columns and three rows, both of which automatically size vertically. Now, we want to start setting up the rest of our page. We'll start by styling our header:

```
#header {
    grid-column: 1; /* location of the element */
    grid-column-span: 4; /* width of the element, in column spans */
    grid-row: 1; /* location of the element */
}
```

From there, we'll work on our second row; we'll call our first element `article`, and the second `sidebar-1` and `sidebar-2`.

```
#article { grid-column: 1; grid-column-span: 2; grid-row: 2; }
#sidebar-1 { grid-column: 3; grid-column-span: 1; grid-row: 2; }
#sidebar-2 { grid-column: 4; grid-column-span: 1; grid-row: 2; }
```

Finally, we'll work on our bottom section. We'll call these `postscript-1` through `postscript-4`.

```
#postscript-1 { grid-column: 1; grid-column-span: 1; grid-row: 3; }
#postscript-2 { grid-column: 2; grid-column-span: 1; grid-row: 3; }
#postscript-3 { grid-column: 3; grid-column-span: 1; grid-row: 3; }
#postscript-4 { grid-column: 4; grid-column-span: 1; grid-row: 3; }
```

As you can see, this new module is fairly easy when compared to Susy above—especially in terms of defining your grids and placing information. However, this specification is currently only available in the IE10 Platform Preview, which means that you can't actually use it right now. And that paradoxically, there's something that IE is ahead of the curve on. I'll give you a moment to absorb that.

Going Deeper: CSS Layout and Grid Systems

Although it's hard to feel that CSS as a layout engine has found its way yet, there's a lot to be hopeful for. People are working hard around the world to find options that work in multiple browsers, and new options are turning up all the time. If you want to learn more about grids and CSS layout, the following resources might prove useful:

- Vinh, Khoi. "Ordering Disorder: Grid Principles for Web Design." New Riders, 2011.
- Gasston, Peter. "The Future of CSS Layouts." .net Magazine. August 3, 2011. *http://www.netmagazine.com/features/future-css-layouts*.
- Boulton, Mark. "Rethinking CSS Grids." From Mark Boulton's blog, August 8, 2011. *http://www.markboulton.co.uk/journal/comments/rethinking-css-grids*
- The w3c's editor's draft for CSS Grid Layout: *http://dev.w3.org/csswg/css3-grid-align/*
- Official documentation on Compass: *http://compass-style.org/*
- Official documentation on Sass: *http://sass-lang.com/*
- The Grid System. Online resource about grids in both print and web design. *http://www.thegridsystem.org/*
- Design by Grid. Articles, tutorials and resources for grids in web design: *http://www.designbygrid.com/*
- The Golden Grid System. I haven't played with this yet, but it looks very promising for responsive grid-based layout: *http://goldengridsystem.com/*
- The 1140 grid, designed by Andy Taylor. Another option for adaptive layout, which starts at 1140px wide and reflows columns down to mobile: *http://cssgrid.net/*
- The Square Grid, designed by Avraham Cornfeld: *http://thesquaregrid.com/*. This is a framework based on 35 equal-width columns. Laura Scott of PingV Creative has also incorporated this grid into a Drupal theme, available at *http://drupal.org/project/squaregrid*.

CHAPTER 7

Setting up Fireworks Templates for Drupal

While the Fireworks templates provided by Drupal firm Chapter Three[*] can provide an excellent starting point for your layouts, you may find that having a predetermined set of styles and pages inhibits your creativity. Even if something's all in Helvetica and isn't meant to be a final layout, it can be easy to get caught up in other priorities, and let the defaults do the heavy lifting. Additionally, while the templates provide a good set of default areas that you'll want to consider for 90% of your Drupal implementations, every project is unique enough that it makes sense to put some thought into how you want to set up your layouts rather than depending on what another design team has done.

Below, I'll outline a simple process for creating your own custom Fireworks templates. This process assumes that you have a basic knowledge of how to use Fireworks; if you haven't used it before and need to learn it, Lynda.com has a Fireworks CS5 training course (see *http://www.lynda.com/Fireworks-CS5-tutorials/essential-training/59962-2 .html*), and the *Adobe Classroom in a Book* series has an excellent book on Fireworks (*http://www.amazon.com/Adobe-Fireworks-CS5-Classroom-Book/dp/0321704487*). The book *Adobe Fireworks CS4 How-To's: 100 Essential Techniques* (*http://www.ama zon.com/Adobe-Fireworks-CS4-How-Tos-Techniques/dp/0321562879/ref=sr_1_2?s= books&ie=UTF8&qid=1315255117&sr=1-2*) deals with the previous version of Fireworks, but still provides an excellent introduction to using the software.

For the purposes of this overview, I'll focus on setting up a layout for *tzk-design.com*, my personal site.

---

[*] Available at *http://www.chapterthree.com/blog/nica_lorber/design_drupal_template_approach* and *http:// www.chapterthree.com/greyboxing*.

Step One: Setting Up the Grid

The first step to efficiently setting up a layout is to start with the basics. What are the basic content areas of the page? How will body text and headlines be dealt with? What about links, lists, etc.? These are collected onto a sample page, and styles are set so they can be reused elsewhere.

We'll start with the page grid. Since I'm using the Omega theme to set up this site, I'll be starting out with the standard 960 24-column grid. Each piece of the grid is 30px wide, colored pink at 20% transparency, and placed with a 10px gutter between each piece. That'll be a layer in my document called "24-column grid," which I'll place at the top of my layers and share with all other pages in my document. Figure 7-1 shows how my layout looks after I've set up the grid.

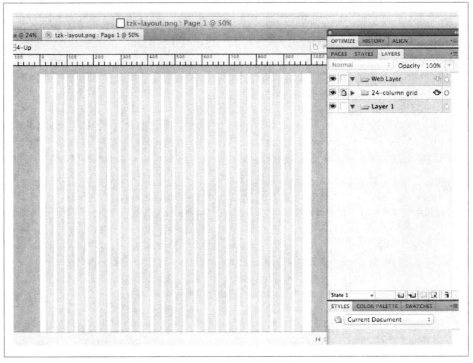

Figure 7-1. After setting up the 24-column grid, we already have a layer set up for our Fireworks template

Step Two: Setting Up the Header

Now that I have my grid in place, I want to take a bit of time thinking through how the navigation will be organized and setting up some type defaults. For that, I'll create a new layer called "header" and bring in my logo, the navigation links and other elements. I can bring these in directly from my style tiles (see Chapter 4, *Using Style Tiles to Explore Design Ideas)*.

With the navigation, I may want to play around with the format of links, text, colors, etc.—but I want to be able to change them across the board when I make edits. For this, I'll convert the navigation to a symbol called "navigation" (do this by selecting the navigation elements, right clicking, and selecting "Convert to Symbol" from the contextual menu). I'll also set up some Styles for the navigation, including the type format for links in their on and off state, and a style for the background of the on state. Figure 7-2 shows what my Layers and Styles palettes look like when I'm done.

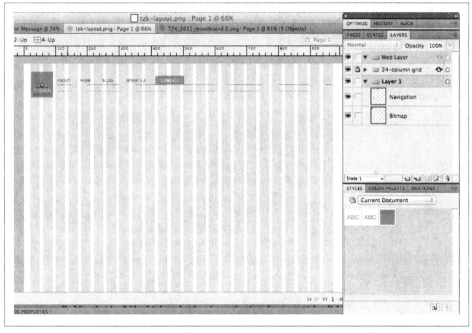

Figure 7-2. Our new navigation, straight from the mood board we created earlier

Once we've created the navigation, we want to make sure that we label our new layer "Header" and share it to all pages in our document. I'll also add a small "Accepting work in:" status message (see Figure 7-3) in the upper-right corner, which will be brought in as a block when I build the site.

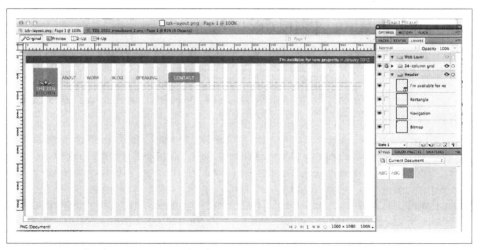

Figure 7-3. Our header is starting to take shape

Step 3: Single Node Page

Now that we have our header in place, we should probably think about how type will look. For this, we'll start with a single node page, which will give us an opportunity to figure out a variety of different type defaults.

The focus of a single node page should be on the legibility of the content on the page. I want to avoid a line length that's too long, so I'll keep my content area at a width of 12 columns, which is about half the page. It's important to test out a couple of different types of copy that could appear in a given text sample, so I'll include a secondary heading, a pullout quote (which I'll convert into a symbol) and some sample body copy. I also want to make sure I plan for titles that might go long, so I'll set my h1 as a two-line title to see how it looks. Finally, each element in my sample copy will have its styles saved in the Styles palette:

- h1: the page title
- p: the body copy
- h2: the secondary title underneath the first paragraph
- blockquote: the pullout quote. The entire block quote is pulled out from the main flow of the text and saved as a symbol

Figure 7-4 shows where we are with our sample node page.

Right now, we're assuming that this page has no sidebar; this means that we're going to end up with a lot of extra space on the right side of the content unless we come up with some sensible margins. Looking at our grid again, I see that the logo is set as a 2-column wide image; let's move the content 2 columns to the right to align with the left

Figure 7-4. Setting up a sample node page to set up our content styles

edge of the navigation. We'll also make the content area wider: 14 columns instead of 12. While I'm at it, I'll create a footer for the page, repeating the three dotted lines I used below the navigation to create a balance to the page, and creating new styles called "footer p" and "footer a" for the Footer text. Figure 7-5 shows where I've landed.

Figure 7-5. Our finished node page

Now that we have an idea of what a node page looks like without a sidebar, it's easy enough to copy this page and use it to create a second template with one sidebar, and another with two sidebars.

Step 4: Single Node Pages with Sidebars

The point of starting off your template with a node page that doesn't have sidebars is this: *you will inevitably have a page like this somewhere on your site.* And many designers, well-meaning as they are, end up forgetting this and assume there will be 1–2 sidebars on the page. As Drupal's default behavior reflows the text to fill the entire page when there are no sidebars, this results in these pages having long and drastically uncomfortable line lengths.

That said, it's safe to assume that most pages will have at least one sidebar, and that the sidebars will contain different types of blocks, for example:

- A list of node titles or categories
- Static text or images
- A tag cloud or something similar
- Callout boxes, like a contact form or customer testimonial

Therefore, while I'm working on my node pages, I should also take a look at how these different types of sidebar blocks will be styled, and how I'll set up both one- and two-sidebar layouts. I'll use my two-sidebar layout as my blog post page, and set up a "recent entries" block, tag cloud, and "about the blog" description block. Because presentations end up being a large part of my work, I'll also put a "recent presentations" block in the right sidebar, with images. This will give me the opportunity to create styles for other blocks that include images. Figure 7-6 shows the result.

Creating the sidebars gives me an opportunity to set up a few more styles, including "sidebar h2" (for block titles), "date callout" for the blog post date and presentation date, "tag cloud" for the links in the cloud, and "a" for links. Note the style names: each style's name is related to a piece of the theme that's going to be styled with CSS later.

Another thing to note here is the placement of blocks: since I'm using Omega as my base theme, viewing my layout on a smaller screen, such as a tablet in portrait mode or a smartphone screen, will cause the blocks to the right of my content area to float underneath the content in the order they appear. As such, I want to make sure that the blocks are placed in order of importance: first the "about" section, then post tags, then recent entries, and finally, presentations. As I build this out, the priorities may change, but for now, this looks good.

Figure 7-6. Our two-sidebar layout contains the info we need, but leaves plenty of room for the blog post, which is the focus of the page

Once we have a two-sidebar page done, it's easy enough to do a one-sidebar page. I'll start by duplicating my two-sidebar layout and removing the right sidebar. Then I'll make the right sidebar just a little bit wider, which will help it fill out more of the page. If we look at Figure 7-7, we'll see where we've gotten with that layout.

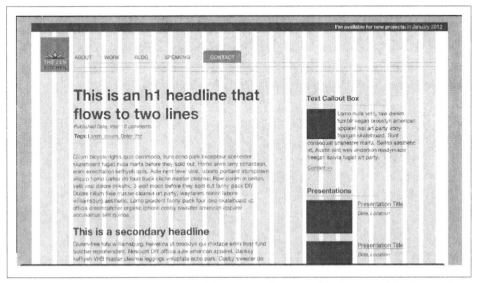

Figure 7-7. Our one-sidebar layout is much less cramped compared to the two-sidebar layout, but is mostly useful when there are just a few things that go on the page aside from content

One of the great things about working in Fireworks—although this is also true of Illustrator and Photoshop—is the ability to easily show and hide layers. In my Fireworks document, I can toggle my grid on to quickly size elements, then toggle it off to see how the overall page looks.

Step 5: Create the Other Pages

Now that I have my basic page structure down, it's time to start looking at the other pages in my site. Working with the styles I've already created (and creating new ones as I need to), I'll create the following pages in my layout:

- Blog listing, with the sidebars as used in my two-sidebar layout
- Category page, based on the blog listing page
- Project page, with associated images and text
- Project listing, with images and a brief project description
- Contact page
- A 404 (page not found) and 403 (access denied) page
- The home page, with associated blocks and callout areas

This should cover most of the pages that I will be setting up in the Drupal implementation, and give me more than enough to work with. Many of the pages will feed each other—for example, my blog listing page will start with my two-sidebar layout, and change the listing, and then the category page will follow from that. However, the project pages, being highly image/case study focused, will require special treatment, including putting some thought into how I'm going to organize the projects, and how they should be displayed. This is where having the real content comes in handy; because I know that the content I'm dealing with in this section is highly visual, I realize that my needs for this particular page will be different than my needs for the blog pages. Figures 7-8 through 7-10 show the approximate layouts that I've created.

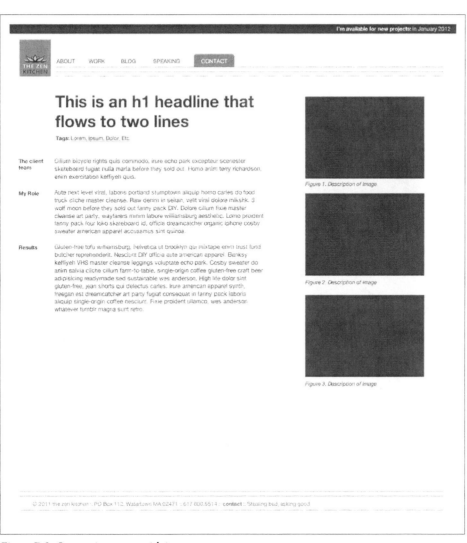

Figure 7-8. Our project page, with images

Figure 7-9. The blog listing, with pager

Figure 7-10. The project listing, grouped into the types of projects I typically work on

Step 6: Step Up the Visuals

Up until this point, with the exception of the logo and header, I've purposely kept the visuals pretty low-key. The purpose of this first phase of design is to focus on the grid and the structure of the page, similar to what I'd do in the wireframing stage. Once I have those standards set, though, it's time to start adding some more interesting visuals to the page.

The first piece is to start adding color. I've already created my color palette and chosen my fonts in the style tiles I created earlier (see Chapter 4), so I'll start by making my headers brown, and setting them in Impressum, the font I've chosen for the headers. I'll do this by selecting the post title on any page, restyling it with my new color and font, selecting it, and then choosing "Redefine Style" from the Styles palette (see Figure 7-11). Once the style is redefined, any instance of that style will have the new attributes I have chosen.

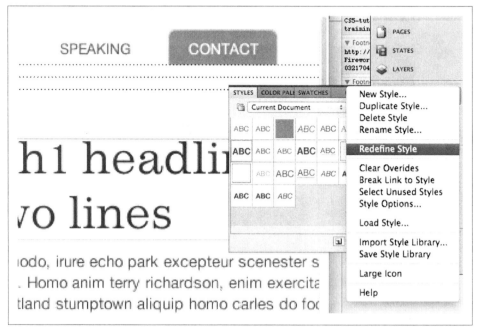

Figure 7-11. Redefining our H1 style. If we look on our pages once the style is redefined, we'll notice that everything has been restyled now

After I've defined my headers, I'll redefine the styles for the other elements of my page using the same process. Add a few flourishes, and we're looking pretty darn good. Figures 7-12, 7-13, and 7-14 show some of my completed pages with the new styles.

Now we have a layout that we can start putting into Drupal. In addition to understanding the basic page structure, we've also started setting up some typographic styles that will guide our design, which will help us make more efficient CSS to code our theme.

Figure 7-12. New blog post page with styles applied. As you can see, I've started to set some visual standards; for example, links in orange and green for subtitles, etc.

In the next section of the book, we'll start looking at how to prototype a site for Drupal. For the purposes of the next section, we'll focus on a different project, called Urban Homesteaders Unite. This project, which I'm collaborating on with my friend Tricia Okin of Papercut, will allow us to get into some much more interesting design challenges, including working with complex Views relationships and customizing profile pages.

Figure 7-13. The project page looks even better, borrowing from the blog page's titles

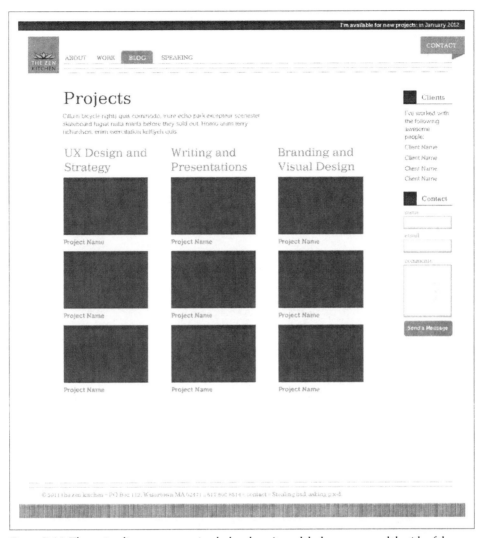

Figure 7-14. The project list stays pretty simple, but doesn't need the banner around the title of the page

PART III

Prototyping, Theming, and Managing your Markup

CHAPTER 8

Paper Prototyping

While prototyping in the browser is useful when you're starting to imagine how a given function or section of a site might work out, it's also a lot of work. If you're not sure about a given bit of design logic, or how a certain piece of the user flow will work out, it could take a lot of time and energy to try to prototype the interaction in Drupal—and if you end up realizing that the solution you've created has usability problems, or is best done another way, it can be frustrating to "throw away" all the work you did.

One way to deal with this uncertainty is by using paper prototypes. Paper gives you the flexibility to move things around when they don't work, or to try out complex interactions, in a way that doesn't require you to throw a bunch of time into code. It also has the benefit of being extremely portable, and it lets you try out ideas on the fly. By showing a paper prototype to a user and having them show you how they would go about completing a given task, you get quick access to usability problems that crop up in your designs. Most importantly, once you discover those problems, *you can get more information about why the problems occurred, and make changes to your prototype on the fly*.

This is the single most important point about paper prototyping. Where a usability test involving a piece of software or a website that's already been built can reveal usability issues that you have to tackle later, in the iteration process, paper prototypes let you find the mistakes and fix them *in front of the user*. Each time you fix something, you get a little bit closer to something that works; and you save yourself a whole lot of headaches and code when it comes time to build things.

When to Use a Paper Prototype

While conceivably, a paper prototype could be used for any application, including a corporate website, they tend to be most useful when the interaction you're trying to create for a user has a bit of complexity to it. Examples include:

- Shopping carts
- Sites in which content categorization is a primary part of the navigation (e.g., higher ed websites, or e-commerce applications)
- Sites that require some type of form entry (log in screens, checkout screens, etc.)

Working with mobile layout (whether you're making a website or an application) is an especially good application of paper prototypes; since the experience of a mobile site needs to be much more concentrated, paper prototypes can help identify which tasks or information are most important to users, and where the frustration patterns come in.

Fidelity

The level of fidelity in a paper prototype can range from printouts of screen layouts or wireframes to hand drawn interfaces. No matter what level of fidelity you end up with, the point is to get something that a user can start interacting with, and being able to show them the interactions that are taking place while they're doing them.

Creating a Paper Prototype

The best place to start is the sketches you've already made—whether they're in a notebook, or done in a program like Fireworks or Balsamiq Mockups. In a YouTube example of a paper prototype test from Blue Duck Labs for a kid's educational website (*http://youtu.be/9wQkLthhHKA*), the examples are mocked up from screen wireframes; in another example from South African UX designer Werner Puchert (*http://youtu.be/y4Wwnt9KIjg*), each aspect of the prototype is sketched by hand. What you decide depends on where you are in the project and what you're comfortable with. At the least, the prototype should have:

- **A place to start**. This could be the home page; it could be a specific section of the site you're focusing on.
- **Somewhere to go**. Each paper prototype should be focused on a specific set of tasks, so make sure that your prototype includes each screen related to that task.
- **An indication of what happens when you go there**. This is the most important part. In a paper prototype, you're trying to assess the interaction that's happening, and make sure that users understand how it is meant to work. Most importantly, users should be able to understand how it works *without you having to tell them*.

The last point is one of the key benefits of keeping paper prototypes low-fidelity. If, for example, a user clicks on a button you weren't expecting them to click on, you need to be able to show them the interaction that will happen when they click on it. If you're keeping to low-fi prototypes, it's much easier to sketch out the interaction on a new piece of paper or a Post-It than it is to anticipate every possible interaction in a given flow for the purposes of a prototype. Or worse—to try making a quick mockup of a new screen in code to print out while the user is waiting. That way leads chaos.

Walking Through the Prototype

It's hard to demonstrate in words exactly how to walk through the prototype with a potential user. In the interview with David Rondeau of InContext Design (see "From the Trenches: David Rondeau, inContext Design" on page 69), he walks through the process that his team uses for working with paper prototypes; however, the following videos can also give you a good visual demonstration of a variety of paper prototype techniques:

- Animating Paper Prototypes: blog post plus video from UK designer Chris Neale: *http://e102.co.uk/?p=3*
- Example Usability Test, from Blue Duck Labs: *http://youtu.be/9wQkLthhHKA*
- Low-Fi Web Prototype II, by Werner Puchert: *http://youtu.be/y4Wwnt9KIjg*
- A few examples from Drupal UX designer Roy Scholten:
  - *http://www.youtube.com/user/royscholten#p/u/1/7VOkLzD3yDs*
  - *http://www.youtube.com/user/royscholten#p/u/10/Yn0ZgKf74xM*
  - *http://www.youtube.com/user/royscholten#p/u/9/Z0UZkkvDTCM*

From the Trenches: David Rondeau, inContext Design

David Rondeau is the Design Chair at InContext Design, a user experience design firm based in Concord, MA (*http://www.incontextdesign.com*). InContext created the Contextual Design process, which is taught at universities all over the world. Paper prototypes are a significant part of the Contextual Design process, meaning that David and his colleagues use them as part of every project.

Dani: What is it that you love so much about paper prototypes? Why do they work so well for you?

David: Paper prototypes are critical for allowing you to validate the structure, basic functions, and the flow of your design, before having to code anything. It works because it's paper, so it's easy to make. There's not a ton of time and overhead involved; people can argue that they can do HTML just as fast, but I don't believe it. Besides, any time you start using a specific tool, you start getting bogged down in details.

Dani: So walk me through the Contextual Design process.

David: In a typical project, we might go out and do 12–30 interviews with people, who are the users of whatever kind of product it is that we're looking at. We consolidate the data, put it all up on a wall, and then we do what we call "walking the wall." We'll walk along the wall, looking at all this data, for a couple of hours, to prime our brains so we understand the user's problems—what they do, what works for them, what doesn't. Then we have our brainstorming session, which we call "visioning."

In visioning, we tell the story of what the future would be based on what we now know. It's wide, it's broad, and we come up with all kinds of cool things that will support the user in ways that haven't been done yet. Once we have that vision, that's when the second half of the project starts.

That's part of the process of using paper prototypes. You have a bunch of ideas, grounded in data. Even with all that data, and with clients in the room who understand the domain, you're still never going to get everything right. Ever. I've been doing design for 20 years, this type of design for 11, and I still have yet to see a perfect first-round paper prototype. There's always something that's not quite right.

Dani: I think that's one of the things that makes paper prototypes so useful. Your first couple of options are never quite right. When you jump straight into code, or even Fireworks, you're tempted not to "waste" the time you just spent.

David: It's not something you feel like you can just throw away. If you've ever read Bill Buxton's book, *Sketching User Interfaces*, this is one of the key things he talks about. What makes something a sketch is that it can be thrown away. Paper prototypes, then, are basically sketches that you have the user do their work in.

*Dani: I have heard the argument that users just don't **get** paper prototypes. These folks believe the only way you can really show an interaction is to show users something that looks the way that it's going to look.*

David: Well, I've been doing them for 11 years, and I can tell you that they work. If someone's suggesting that they don't work, that often means a) they don't understand how to use them, and b) they're trying to test the wrong level of interaction design.

The other reason paper is good is that it's easy to change, and it allows you to co-design in the moment, with the user. The point of the prototype isn't just to validate your ideas, it's to come back with a prototype that's been changed to support the user's work practice. In interviews, a user might say, "Oh, I need it to do this thing," and we didn't put it in the design. Draw some buttons on the prototype, add another piece of paper, and put it in front of the user, and say, "Okay—let's try to use this." You can't do that in HTML. Once you've committed something to code, it's too much work to change it. The user isn't going to sit there and wait for you to make changes to HTML.

Dani: It gives you that chance to validate what you're thinking and say, "does this even work for the people who have to use it?" before you start throwing things into code.

David: I think it's all about using your time wisely. If you think about design, you don't start designing the look of the buttons right away. You have to understand what the system is supposed to do—what are the core functions, what are the key places that you're supposed to go to, and how do you move between those places? Now you have an idea, now, let's go see if this idea actually works for the people that I want to buy this thing.

Dani: So you do all the research, and now you're at a point where you have to make a design from that research. Now you're going to start sketching out the interface, looking at the different options. Do you start with just one paper prototype and test that, or do you try a couple of options?

David: No, we always test one. The caveat is that there may be some parts in that one that we want to test a couple of options for; but we typically do no more than two.

Dani: How do you test it?

David: It's a two hour interview, usually two people go into it. One person runs the interview/prototype, the other takes notes, since it's too hard to do both at the same time. We'll go to the person's work, because their office is where they do all their work, it's where they might have cheat sheets, notes, people that they talk to to help them get their work done—things you'd never find out if you met them in a Starbucks. They also need to have their computer, because they may need to access their work so they can reference things, etc.

We go in, talk to them for a little while and ask questions for the first 15 minutes or so: what's their work? What do they do? Mind you, these are usually people that we've already interviewed in our initial research. We already understand their "work;" what we're looking for is hooks—real instances of work they just finished or need to do— so we can have them re-do that work in the prototype.

Once we find those hooks, we'll stop and introduce them to the paper prototype. We'll give them a brief intro to the prototype, but we don't give specific details or show them how to use it. We'll say something like, "okay, you were talking about this specific piece of work [the hook] that you do; how would you do that here?" Then we give them a marker or a pen, and tell them "this is your new mouse; this is your new keyboard," and tell them that they can "click" wherever they want on the paper, and then we'll show you what happens.

Dani: Are there any pitfalls to testing the prototype with users?

David: One of the key things you don't want to do is what we call a "demo," which is more like putting it in front of someone and showing them what it does—"Isn't my baby beautiful? Don't you love it?" If you do that, you can't be sure they will give you an honest answer. They'll tell you what they think, which is not always what they need. So if you get them grounded in a real case of their actual work that they've done or that they need to do, then you can talk to them about why they need something. You get the why, not just the what.

Often, we'll be going through the paper prototype, and they'll see some other piece of information or functionality, and they'll say, "Oh, what does that do?" We'll say, "I don't know; why don't you click on it and we'll find out." They click on it, and say, "I could use that." We could just capture that as a validation of one of our concepts— but it's not really a validation because we don't understand why they want it. So we always ask why, or better yet, offer a hypothesis to the user and let them react to it. If you're wrong, they'll tell you, and if you're right, you'll be able to tell right away.

If you say, "Oh—do you need that for this kind of a thing?" they'll either say, "Uh... yeah..." and you ask, "When was the last time you did that?" and they say, "I don't know... six months ago, maybe?" that's really a "No." But if they say, "I did that twice last week," we'll ask more questions. "What did you need? What did you do?"

You want to give them the ability to tell you, but you can't ask too many open-ended questions, because the users—being nice people—want to please you, so they'll make stuff up if they think that's what you want to hear. So if I say, "Do you want that because you need it for X," this isn't made-up stuff, right? They can say, "No, that's stupid. I never do that," or they go, "Yeah, yeah, that's exactly what I need."

Other Types of Prototypes

While paper prototypes are useful when you're working with users face to face, sometimes, that's not an option. How do you rapidly create a prototype you can test remotely without having to jump into Drupal development?

Enter an entire world of digital prototyping software. With these applications, once you get over the initial learning curve, you can create hotspots in your layouts, link them to other pages in your prototype, and mimic a wide range of responses to user inputs. You can test the prototypes in person, or use screen sharing/recording software like Silverback (*http://silverbackapp.com/*) to test your work with people from their own computers.

If you're already using Adobe Fireworks for creating your wireframes or design layouts (see Chapter 7), you can incorporate Hot Spots in your Fireworks layouts to link areas of the layout with other pages in your layout, and export the file as a clickable prototype. Other options for clickable prototypes include:

Axure

Axure (*http://www.axure.com/*) is a desktop program for Mac and Windows, favored by a number of UX designers. The program also has a number of specialized widgets (UX symbols and images) available for free on their website for customizing your prototypes. In addition to being able to create a complete clickable prototype in one document, Axure also allows you to easily create user flows (to show task flows for specific screens) and include them in the prototype. It also allows you to annotate any area of the prototype with notes on functionality, requirements, etc. —and output a detailed functional specification in Word with the click of a button. If you're working with a team to implement your designs, the time savings you get from specification export alone are invaluable.

Justinmind

Another multiplatform desktop option. Justinmind (*http://www.justinmind.com/*) and Axure both come with a hefty pricetag—\$495–\$600.

AppSketcher

Another desktop choice, with a price tag under $200 (*http://www.appsketcher* *.com/*).

HotGloo

HotGloo (*https://www.hotgloo.com/*) is a web-based service available for a monthly subscription depending on how much you use the service.

Pencil Project

Pencil Project (*http://pencil.evolus.vn/en-US/Home.aspx*) is a plugin for Firefox that will let you build prototypes from within the browser itself. It's also one of the few free options for digital prototyping I've come across.

CHAPTER 9

Breaking Down a Layout for Drupal Implementation

The two most important parts of working in Drupal, in terms of creating and implementing layouts for a given page, are figuring out where the content in a given layout is coming from and how to manage the code that Drupal is creating. This is, arguably, the biggest difference between building sites in Drupal and building them with HTML. Whereas it's fairly straightforward to mock up a page in HTML once you have an idea of what it should look like, everything that goes into your Drupal site comes from somewhere in the site's database; your code simply tells Drupal how to render the content it pulls from that database.

Content in a Drupal layout can come from any number of places.

Nodes

Any individual piece of content, in Drupal terms, is called a "node," and it's displayed using a file called *node.tpl.php*. If you're dealing with the layout of a single page and are only concerned with how the actual page content is displayed, you're likely dealing with *node.tpl.php*.

While *node.tpl.php* can help you control certain aspects of how Drupal displays individual nodes—for example, if you want to move the page title, or change the markup that controls the node's container—if your content type has custom fields, as many content types do, you'll want to manage those in the *Manage Display* tab, available by going into the admin area for your content type. From there, you can manage how fields are organized on the page, how and if their labels are displayed alongside the field, and even the format of the field display. For more information on managing content types and fields, check out the *Planning and Managing Drupal Projects* guide. The Practical Example in Chapter 12 also includes an example of setting up custom fields for a content type.

Blocks

Blocks are, essentially, little bits of content that you can put anywhere you want to in your Drupal page. A block can come from anywhere—not only can you create your own blocks through the blocks administration screen *(Structure→Blocks)*, but many modules, such as Views and Drupal's Menu system, create blocks for you that you can then place on your site. A good rule of thumb is this: if something's going into a sidebar or footer, or it's not part of the main content, it's likely coming from a block.

Views

Views helps you create lists of content to put in various places on your site. As you will see in the practical examples in Chapters 12 and 13, I used Views to create a custom "Who's Hosting" block for my *Event* page, with user profile information based on a User reference field. I also used it to create a block of related events for the sidebar, and a list of categories for events with associated images. Views works by setting up your defaults (what Views is pulling out of the database) and parsing it into different displays depending on your needs. Anywhere you have a list of content, you likely have a View.

For example, Figure 9-1 shows the home page of our site for *Urban Homesteaders Unite*.

If I break this down according to the numbers that I've annotated on my layout, I'll see:

- 1, 2, 4, 5, 6, 7, and 8 are all blocks.
- 2, 7, and 8 are blocks built with Views.
- There's no actual node content on the home page.
- 3 is a menu, and comes from the Menu core system.

There's no hard and fast way to know exactly where a bit of content is coming from on the page (for example, depending on the regions in your theme, block #6 could actually be coming in as content from the home page; I'm creating it as a block because it's easier to theme that way), but there's a few things that it's safe to assume:

- Anything that is in the menu bar comes from the menu system.
- Anything that looks like a list of content, users, or taxonomy terms comes from Views displays.
- Anything that is contained within its own little box on the page is likely a Block.

Once you have an idea of where content comes from, it's easier to figure out how you're going to put things into Drupal. Even if you're just creating a layout for someone else to implement, knowing how things are going to be implemented, and learning the design patterns that Drupal gives you will make your job infinitely easier.

Figure 9-1. *Our rough homepage mockup for UHU, with annotations*

Remember: an important part of good design is understanding the constraints that you're dealing with, and how much you can stretch against those constraints. You'll hear this from me several times before this book is done, but trust me: going *with* Drupal, rather than *against* it, will take you far. And you can still do gorgeous design. Really.

CHAPTER 10

Working with Base Themes

Back when I was using WordPress to build most of my sites, the process of theming (i.e., applying the look and feel to a website) was relatively simple. I'd mock up the design that I was thinking about, head over to *wordpress.org*, and find a theme that had the same basic structure as the site I was designing. Then I'd hack apart the files, customizing it with my own CSS and images. Changing the HTML output was pretty simple as well; as long as I could pick out the few bits of PHP code that were making the site render content and not mess with them too much, it wasn't a big deal to customize container names or change the format of a given page.

When I did my first Drupal site, back when Drupal 6 was still relatively new, I thought the process would be about the same. I mocked up my template, went to *drupal.org*, and started searching for a contributed theme that looked sort of like what I was going for. Then I started trying to customize it according to what I'd mocked up.

I cried my way through that first site. And drank more coffee than I care to talk about.

As I started to chat with other designers about this problem, I realized I wasn't alone. Drupal's theme layer is impressive, flexible, and powerful; it's also confusing as hell until you get used to it. The biggest layer of confusion is this: while in WordPress, it's generally fine to download a theme package and start hacking it up to customize it, you don't want to do that in Drupal. Why? Because Drupal keeps tabs on that theme file, and includes it in any updates you make to your site's code. This means that any customizations you make will be *gone* as soon as you update the code. All of them. Really.[*]

The other problem with hacking themes directly is making sense of the code. While some themes allow you to make any customizations you need directly in the template files (files that end with *tpl.php*), many advanced themes put most of their theme overrides directly into *template.php*, a set of PHP functions that controls various aspects of the way Drupal renders the page. In fact, I've seen themes where everything—including how 960 grid classes are rendered—is thrown into *template.php*. This means that,

---

[*] All. Of. Them.

unless you're really cozy with PHP and don't mind spending your time writing theme functions, you'll be lost the moment you try to customize a theme.

This is where choosing a good base theme comes in handy. A *base theme*, in Drupal terms, is a theme that contains minimal styling, a good number of templates (*.tpl.php* files) that you can duplicate into your child theme and customize, and renders code in a way that you can customize via CSS. The base theme, ideally, handles most of the heavy lifting in terms of rendering the page layout, and setting reasonable defaults for font sizes, form elements, and the like. By creating a *child theme* derived from this base, you create all your customizations in a separate set of files within the */sites/all/themes* folder, which keeps your custom code safe—and helps you debug issues without having to worry about the base theme getting wrecked. It also has the key benefit of letting someone else (the theme maintainer) worry about updates to the theme; since your customizations will mostly involve CSS and the occasional *.tpl.php* file, they won't often be completely borked by security updates.

How to Choose a Base Theme

Choosing a base theme is often a matter of personal preference. *Drupal.org* offers quite a few to choose from, and every site builder has their favorite. Whichever you choose, make sure that your base theme:

Has a way of dealing with code and CSS files that makes sense to you
> If you've never worked with Drupal themes before, it might seem like none of them are organized in ways that make sense; however, some themes are more confusing than others. For me, I prefer to avoid themes that throw all of the page rendering information into functions in template.php; while I don't mind dealing with some PHP, I also avoid themes that separate each aspect of the page into separate CSS files that you have to sort through (I'm looking at you, Zen).

Spits out relatively clean code
> You aren't always going to be able to find the ultimate, beautiful semantic markup that you might want from a base theme, but you can at least get close. If you can't get exactly the code you want out of your base theme, there are a couple of modules that can help; check out Chapter 14 for examples.

Has enough tpl.php files that you can customize the code easily if you need to
> At the very least, a good base theme should have its own version of *page.tpl.php*, *block.tpl.php*, and *node.tpl.php* available for you to customize. You may not need to customize it in your child theme, but having it there is incredibly useful for the possibility that you will need to.

Whichever base theme you select, you'll want to save into */sites/all/themes* and enable it in your *Appearance* settings (Figure 10-1).

It's very likely that you'll end up trying out a few base themes before you settle on one you like. On the recommendation of a few friends in the Drupal community, I tried

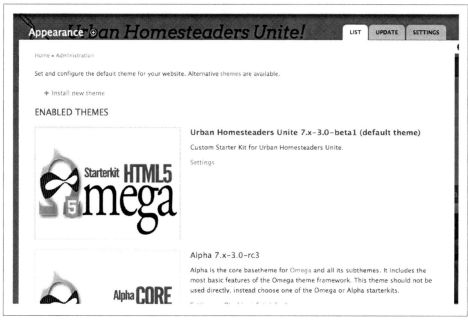

Figure 10-1. The Appearance settings page (Appearance) lets you enable themes in your Drupal site, and set the default theme for your particular site

Zen (*drupal.org/project/zen*) a few times before realizing that I couldn't make sense of it. After giving up Zen, I switched to the NineSixty base theme (*drupal.org/project/ ninesixty*), which is based on the 960 grid system (960.gs). NineSixty was, and still is, one of my favorites to work with; the grid system gives me the ability to quickly make layout adjustments, and the code is cleaner than many base themes that I've worked with, particularly once I started creating my own starter kit with most of the extraneous <divs> deleted.

However, in the last year or so, as HTML5 and responsive design has become more of a priority, I've started experimenting with Omega (*drupal.org/project/omega*). Omega is an HTML5-based theme with three versions of the 960.gs grid at the ready and a completely responsive layout (which resizes according to your browser window.) While it's not without its stuff to figure out (including a whole lotta *template.php*), one of my favorite things about Omega is the ability to customize the grid for each section of the site. For example, on Urban Homesteaders Unite, I use a 12-column grid on the header, but a 16-column grid in the Content region, which gives me a bit more flexibility in the layout.

Another nice thing about Omega is the ability to update my page defaults through a GUI in the theme settings page (Figure 10-2). This frees me to experiment with different layouts as I need to, without having to search through code and tweak grid numbers here and there. I don't know if it's faster than tweaking code directly, but it's certainly a bit more idiot-proof.

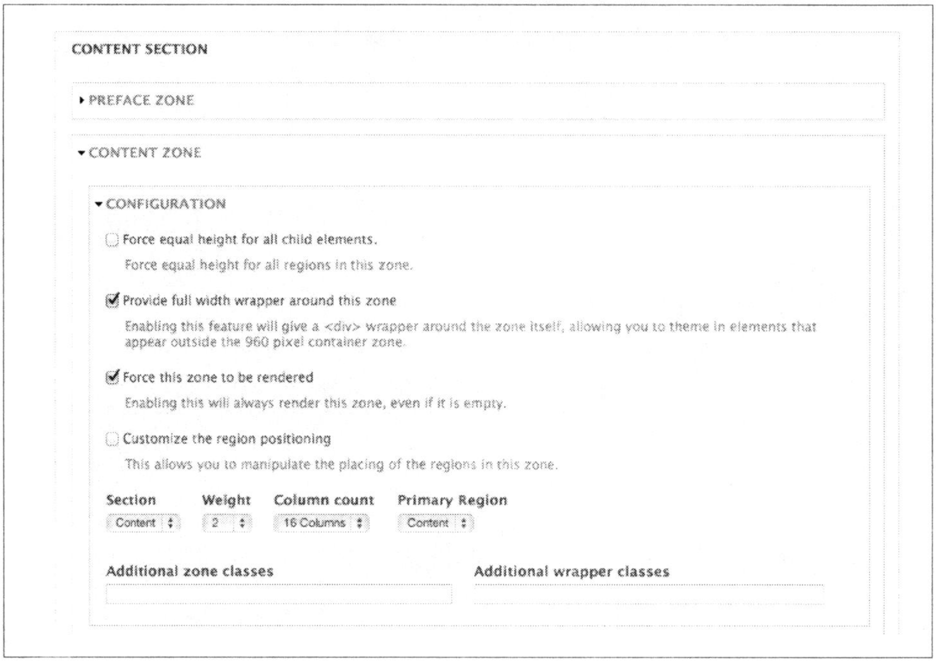

Figure 10-2. Updating the Content region defaults in Omega's snazzy region settings GUI

Other Base Themes to Try

Now that I've given you my favorites, here are some other base themes to try, based on recommendations from friends in the Drupal community:

Square Grid (drupal.org/project/squaregrid)
> Square Grid, created by PingV Creative's Laura Scott, uses the Square Grid framework (mentioned in the chapter on using grids) as a base. This 35-column layout gives you quite a bit of flexibility in organizing your site's blocks and columns, and like Omega, it also takes mobile-first layout into consideration.

Tao (drupal.org/project/tao)
> Tao is a base theme that simply resets a lot of Drupal's default page rendering behavior. The goal of it is to sit back and let your subtheme do its job. It does assume a focus on preprocessors (i.e., setting up things in template.php), which might mean that you have to deal with a lot of PHP and theme functions, but it also provides many advantages, such as sensible code to start working with.

Mothership (drupal.org/project/mothership)
> This theme does what it can to strip out many of the extra <divs> and classes that tend to plague Drupal's way of displaying data. This gives you the ability to start

your theme with a clean slate, and creates nice, semantic markup. It even helps you get rid of the crazy extra code that Views can tend to spit out. We'll chat about that a bit more in Chapter 13, which is all about managing the code that Views gives you.

Zen (drupal.org/project/zen)

If you spend any time in the Drupal community, frankly, you're going to hear a lot of people recommending Zen. In fact, it's such a common base theme that many people who start working with Drupal start out working with the Zen theme, often on the recommendation of a developer they know. As you might have guessed from my comments above, I'm not a huge fan of Zen, but I include it because you'll probably hear about it at some point. One thing it does well is produce well-ordered code; unfortunately, it suffers from many extra <div> tags, and multiple CSS files that handle different aspects of page layout, which can be confusing for new themers.

Creating a Child Theme

Once you've got your base theme downloaded and set up, you have to set up a child theme to put all your customizations into. Some themes, such as Zen and Omega, come with a set of starter kits that you can simply copy into your */sites/all/themes* folder and rename; with other themes, you may have to copy the files you need manually into a new folder. To start with, all child themes should contain three files:

- A **blank** *template.php* file, which will eventually hold any theme functions that you decide to put into it. Note that this file should be *blank* initially; copying the *template.php* file from your base theme will cause errors when you try to access your site.
- A *THEMENAME.info* file, which you can copy from the base theme.
- A *styles.css* (or something similar) file, which will be referenced in your theme's *.info* file and contain all of the CSS customizations for your child theme.

If you plan on overriding any of the base theme's *tpl.php* files, you can also copy those into your child theme. However, generally, I avoid doing that unless I need to create a new template region, or change the base theme's grid layout.

To create your child theme, you'll start by modifying the theme's *.info* file. The *.info* file defines the page regions, CSS and Javascript files that your theme will use. For example, here's part of the content of the *.info* file that comes with Omega's HTML5 starter kit:[†]

[†] If you're interested in trying out Omega, it's recommended that you work with one of the starter kits that come with the theme *instead* of trying to copy the one that comes with Omega itself. Omega's *.info* file is copious and full of interesting settings that don't need to be copied into your child theme.

```
name = Omega
description = <a href="http://drupal.org/project/omega">Omega</a> extends the Omega
theme framework with some additional features and makes them availabe to its subthemes.
This theme should not be used directly, instead choose one of the Omega or Alpha
starterkits.
core = 7.x
engine = phptemplate
screenshot = screenshot.png
version = 3.x
base theme = alpha

; REGIONS
; REQUIRED CORE REGIONS
regions[page_top] = Page Top
regions[page_bottom] = Page Bottom
regions[content] = Content

; END REQUIRED CORE REGIONS
regions[user_first] = User Bar First
regions[user_second] = User Bar Second
regions[branding] = Branding
regions[menu] = Menu
```

If you've copied your base theme's *.info* file into your child theme's folder, you can generally delete everything in the "stylesheets" and "scripts" sections. The information on whatever *regions* your base theme has identified, however, must stay where they are. Regions are specific areas on the page where you can place content—usually through the Blocks administration (*Structure→Blocks* or, if you're using the Context module [*drupal.org/project/context*], through the Context administration). There's a couple of things you need to remember when modifying your *.info* file:

- As mentioned before, any regions your base theme has defined should *stay in the file*. Any regions that are set up in your child theme's template files, but aren't listed in its *.info* file, could break your theme.

- Themes have two names: the Machine Name and the Human-Friendly Name. Machine Names are always written in lowercase, with underscores instead of spaces (i.e, my_awesome_theme), while Human Friendly Names can have upper-case letters, spaces, etc. (i.e., My Awesome Theme).

- The top bit of information (name, description, core version, engine, etc.) should stay at the top of the page. These are required by Drupal to make the theme work. Most of it should stay the same as what's in your base theme, with the exception of the name and description.‡

- Additionally, you want to include base theme = MACHINE_NAME underneath the top set of descriptive information. In the Omega example above, you can see that Omega is using a theme called Alpha as its base theme; if you were creating a child

‡ If you want to learn more about what goes into a theme's *.info* file, check out *http://drupal.org/node/171205*, which has a complete list of the types of information you can put in there.

theme from Omega, you would change that text to `base theme = omega`. Likewise, if you were creating a child theme based on NineSixty, which doesn't have its own base theme, you'd add `base theme = ninesixty` to your child theme's *.info* file.

Once you've updated the descriptive information and identified the base theme that you're working with, you want to include any stylesheets or Javascript files that you want to include in your theme.

For example, here's the updated *.info* file for my Urban Homesteaders Unite theme (which was created with the HTML5 starter kit that comes with Omega):

```
name = Urban Homesteaders Unite
description = Custom Starter Kit for Urban Homesteaders Unite.
core = 7.x
engine = phptemplate
screenshot = screenshot.png
base theme = omega

; REQUIRED CORE REGIONS
regions[page_top] = Page Top
regions[page_bottom] = Page Bottom
regions[content] = Content

; OPTIONAL STYLESHEETS
css[mobile.css][name] = Mobile Styles
css[mobile.css][description] = Your custom CSS for the mobile version of your website
(mobile first).
css[mobile.css][options][weight] = -89

css[styles.css][name] = Main Styles
css[styles.css][description] = Your main custom CSS file.
css[styles.css][options][weight] = 10
```

From there, you should be able to enable your theme through the *Appearance* menu, set it as the default, and plug away at your styles.css file (Figure 10-3).

Figure 10-3. Setting our theme defaults

Other Things You Should Know About Base Themes

Now that you've gotten the hang of editing your theme's *.info* file and making a child theme, there are a couple of other things that you should bear in mind when working:

Clear the Theme Registry!

Any time you add a new element to your *.info* file—whether it's to add a new region to your page, or add a new stylesheet (for example, I sometimes like to add a separate stylesheet for the navigation on sites with complex navigation styles), *you must clear your theme registry*. Sometimes, for really sticky issues, you can also try clearing all of the caches. You can clear all caches by going into *Configuration→Performance* and pressing the "Clear all Caches" button. If you're feeling super nerdy, you can also use the command `drush cc all` to clear the caches from within Drush, the command line tool for Drupal. We'll discuss Drush in the next book, *Drupal Development Tricks for Designers* (cue evil laughing).

> You don't have to clear the cache every time you do something simple, like changing the CSS in your theme; but if you make a change and nothing happens, clearing the cache will often help.

Working with Regions

Regions are Drupal's way of laying out containers for content in a given theme. Many themes, such as Bartik and Omega, come with a copious volume of regions—all with odd names like "Triptych," "Postscript," and "Preface"—for your block organization pleasure. This is, in fact, one of the things you want in a base theme—the more regions you have, even if you use none of them, the more flexibility you have in your layout. The trick is to understand what the regions mean, and to use your layout to guide where you put things.

In Drupal 6, your theme's regions would be overlaid directly in the Blocks administration screen. In Drupal 7, things are different. If you look at your Blocks administration screen *(Structure→Blocks)*, you'll see this link: "Demonstrate block regions (theme name)" (Figure 10-4).

If you click that link, you'll see a page that shows all the regions you have available in your theme (Figure 10-5).

As you can see, there's a lot to work with here; however, it's not always easy to remember which region is where, or how things are going to show up. For that reason, I tend to keep either a print or a sketch of my theme's regions in my project file as I'm working. If I lose track of something, I just refer to my printout, and I'm good to go.

Figure 10-4. If you go into Blocks administration, you'll see a link that will let you show the theme's associated regions

Figure 10-5. Theme regions for our Omega theme

Please, Tell Me More!

We've really just scratched the surface of working with Base themes in Drupal 7. If you're itching (and I just know that you are) to learn more, check out *http://drupal.org/node/225125*, where the lovely folks in the Drupal community have running documentation on how to create a subtheme, with commentary. You can also add comments and questions to the documentation page, simply by logging in with your Drupal.org account.

CHAPTER 11

Prototyping in the Browser

Some designers, like independent designer and web strategist Jason Pamental (*thinkinginpencil.com*) interviewed below, prefer to do site prototyping directly in the browser. For Pamental, doing things this way gives you the opportunity to see things as they actually behave in the browser, rather than mocking things up in Photoshop or Fireworks only to spend hours explaining to clients why the designs changed once they were implemented in Drupal.

The trick to this approach, however, is not falling into the trap of simply decorating on top of what Drupal gives you—but rather, as Todd Nienkerk suggests in his Drupalcon session, *Don't Design Websites, Design Web SYSTEMS!*,[*] letting Drupal's default behavior simply provide a guide your design decisions.

When a site doesn't require a lot of complex interaction (for which I do paper- or Axure-based prototypes) I'm a big fan of the "sketch, quickly wireframe, then start prototyping in Drupal" approach. Being able to see how the interactions I'm designing can be implemented in Drupal helps me make smarter decisions about layout and functionality, because it helps me make sure that what I'm proposing can actually be done. In practice, it often looks like this:

- I'll create a bunch of sketches for possible page layouts, interactions, etc. and choose 1–2 to start wireframing.
- I'll create wireframes for the 1–2 best options, and talk them over with the project team.
- I'll work those wireframes into some kind of (non-Drupal) prototype, so the project team can see how the interactions should work.

---

[*] Check out the slide deck at *http://fourkitchens.com/presentations*.

- Those will be iterated until we figure out the best solution for what we're dealing with.
- I'll either start working on prototyping my assumptions in Drupal, or I'll work with the team's developer to start prototyping right away while I work on the next area of functionality/content that needs fleshing out.

This is also one of the key reasons why I break up work plans into specific functional areas of the site. It helps me focus the team's energy on getting one specific area working before we go too deeply into the next area. This approach can be called many things; some think of it as Agile (from the software programming methodology), others call it Lean (from the Lean Startup concept).[†] I tend to think of it as a Lean hybrid; the point is less about getting a Minimum Viable Product up and running within a couple of weeks, and more about being able to quickly get your head around the various complexities of a project, create a bunch of hypotheses to test based on your research, and start seeing how those hypotheses play out as quickly as you can.

From the Trenches: Jason Pamental, independent web strategist

Dani: You've mentioned to me that you prefer to prototype in the browser, rather than in layout comps or sketches. Can you talk a bit more about that?

Jason: The main reason is that, when you prototype in the browser, you can see what it really looks like. It doesn't matter what tricks you have in Photoshop, it's never going to translate exactly into how a web page will behave. So, over the years, I've started to see that, if you have a good base theme, or a handle on writing HTML, you get to a place much faster where you can actually explore behavior—especially when you're putting it right into a content management system. So you can explore more of the real life of a website quickly, rather than trying to mock up every different state of an interaction.

Dani: How do you ideate something like that—do you go straight to code, or do you start with sketches, and then move to code later?

Jason: In terms of the actual design process, there's always work that goes on in Photoshop or Illustrator. But oftentimes, that comes after a prototype's been built. We tend to have this "sandbox" version of a website, that's been built out with all of the main pages, and some of the default users there already. It's really quick to play with things, and think about "How am I going to search?" and "How am I going to play with these things?" Once it's time to go into the look and feel, you have all the real stuff there to play with. Even as you're opening Photoshop or Illustrator, you know the real things that you have to be concerned with—the buttons, navigation elements, and the real content on a page, etc.

But even with that, there's pages and pages of sketches, notes and things like that from early on in the process, especially for something complicated.

[†] For more information on the Lean Startup movement, check out *http://theleanstartup.com/*.

Dani: The flow that I've been moving towards lately is sketch, maybe wireframe a couple of pages, but then start prototyping in Drupal quickly so I can see how things are falling, and how something's going to be implemented. The question I always ask myself is: how much of that workflow is based on the fact that I'm a team of 1–3, as opposed to being one piece of a larger team? I notice with larger teams, they do often have more clearly defined roles, so there's not as much concern about whether you specifically can implement something, but more about whether it can be implemented by the team. Have you had experience with that?

Jason: I've worked on teams of varying sizes, from just me to managing a group of 3–5 people to being a creative director at a company in Boston with 30 developers and a team of 6 designers. I've never been a big fan of having a person for every possible task and isolating the work that they're doing. It's never seemed to work well.

Especially with a platform like Drupal at your disposal—even doing the site for CVS/CareMark, which is a pretty significant project, it was still a team of 5–6 core people. There was a designer, there was a researcher and information architect, there was me and a couple of developers who were helping me. That was pretty much it.

Dani: That's one of the benefits of Drupal. There's so much that's built for you that it's easier to make big websites with fewer people. I don't think it makes it any less complicated, but I do think it allows you to focus on more important parts of the experience than what the code is going to look like.

Jason: Exactly, and that's one of my favorite things about it. It lets you be a team that is iterative and reactive far more easily than when you have each person in their own separate role. I keep thinking of these companies that push development offshore, or to a partner company, where you have this enforced wall between design and architecture. Maybe there's some prototyping, but the real development happens somewhere else. In those cases, there's no way to just sit down with someone and discuss something, and then react to it right away.

Dani: While you're prototyping in the browser, do you find that there are any moments where you find yourself leaning on Drupal's defaults a bit too heavily?

Jason: That's an easy trap to fall into. Because you know something works, so you put your attention to something else, and it's not necessarily that it works in the best way. I think that's a constant challenge, and not one that's so difficult to overcome if you work smartly. One of the things that I have enjoyed about the process of working on the platform we've built for SchoolYard is that there's a common base point we're starting with. Every project, we get to smooth off more of those rough corners.

I think that when you build up this set of defaults—this set of modules that you always use, this point from which you always start the process—it lets you build up these layers of sophistication. You can start building all these little things that add up to a much more refined experience. That's where taking the time to get to know the platform and just look for stuff and see what's out there—every time you do another project, it just gets better and better.

Dani: How do you document that?

Jason: In part, it's frozen in this starter kit website that I start from every time I start a new project. Periodically I'll go in there and update the modules, and every time I see something interesting I make sure I throw it in there.

That, and blog posts. I do a lot of that. If I figure out some weird challenge, I take notes in Evernote as I figure it out, I make sure I copy down all the steps, and I add in all the things that I have found, and I stick it up on my blog.

CHAPTER 12

Practical Example #1: Using Views to Enhance a Layout

By now, we've had a chance to look at sketching and wireframing designs, creating style tiles and layouts to explore design directions, and different options for prototyping and iterating on those designs. So what happens when you're dealing with a design that's already been created, and you're getting ready to put it into Drupal? Understanding how Drupal stitches pages together can help you find the holes in implementation, and even help you improve the original layout. As an example, let's take this single event page created by Tricia for the Urban Homesteaders Unite site, as shown in Figure 12-1.

The original layout for this page, created before the project was going to be built in Drupal, was inspired by the way that Eventbrite.com displays events. At first glance, this page would be pretty easy to build in Drupal.

But what if we could make it even better?

To do that, we need to consider a couple of things based on the overall vision for the site (a way to get urban homesteaders together for different events), and the way that Drupal will be organizing the site's content:

- Each event is created by a user of the site who is also the host of the event.
- Each user will have their own profile, with contact information, a brief bio, and a link to things they've done on the site.
- Given these two things, what if, rather than having users repeat their contact information as part of each event, you could pull it directly from the host's user profile? This would allow potential attendees put a face to the event, and learn more about the person who's about to teach them this stuff?

This is the type of situation where getting things into Drupal early makes the most sense. The greybox comp in Figure 12-2 shows a rough idea of what we're going to put together.

Figure 12-1. Original design comp for an individual event page on Brooklyn Homesteaders Unite

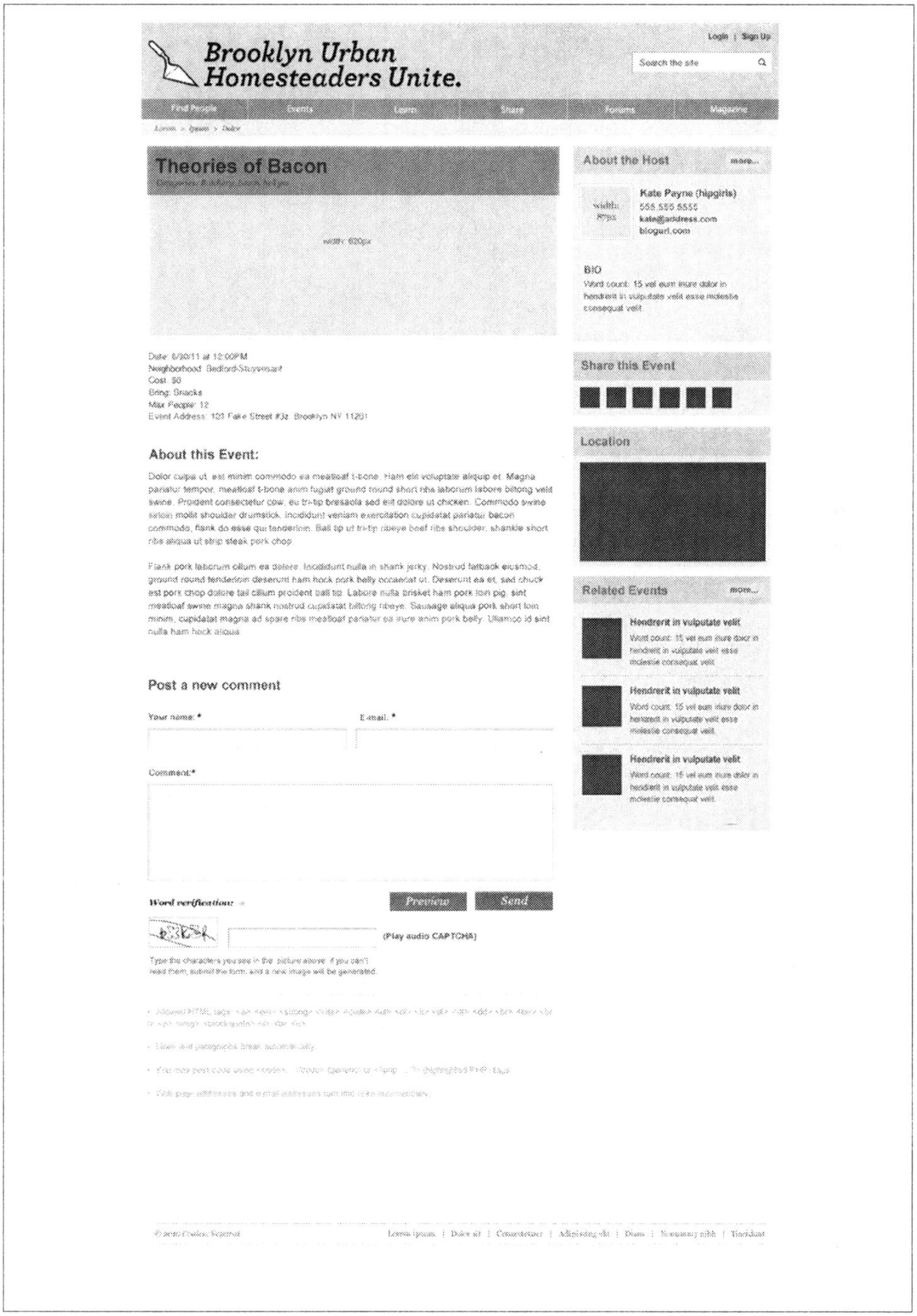

Figure 12-2. A new mockup for the Event page, taking into account the ability to automatically feed in the host's bio information

By starting to prototype this directly in Drupal, we can work out the kinks in our design early, before they cause problems later on.

But I'm Not a Developer—What if I Don't Want to Code?

Admittedly, much of this approach requires a certain willingness to work directly in Drupal, which may (and usually does) mean touching code. The bad news is that if you want to build sites in Drupal, but you don't want to figure out how to deal with the code, you essentially have two options:

- **Partner up with a good developer**. You can meet them all over the place, from local Drupal meetups to online at *groups.drupal.org*. Occasionally, you can even find Drupal developers on Twitter simply by asking a question with the hashtag #Drupal. If you're feeling brave and super-nerdy, you can also check out Drupal folks on various IRC channels.[*]

- **Don't create the site**. I'm serious. If you don't want to deal with code, and you aren't willing to pay a developer, you shouldn't be doing things in Drupal. Many folks don't want to hear this, but it's the truth.

This said, if you're willing to learn, and you don't mind spending a bit of time messing around, you'll find that prototyping directly into Drupal isn't without its headaches, but it's often easier than you may have thought. In some cases, it doesn't even require you to step into code at all.

Here's how I set up the configuration for this crazy-awesome event page in Drupal 7.

Step 1: Create the "Event Categories" Taxonomy Vocabulary

Taxonomy, for those who haven't learned a lot of DrupalSpeak™, is how Drupal categorizes content. Each taxonomy vocabulary is a set of categories, or tags, that you can apply to one or several types of content. In previous versions of Drupal, you could create vocabularies as you needed them, by creating a vocabulary and selecting which content types the vocabulary could be associated with. This was easier in some respects, but could turn complicated as new content types were added.

In Drupal 7, taxonomy vocabularies are treated very differently. Rather than creating the vocabulary after the content type, you create it *before* you create the fields for a content type, and then add a "term reference" field that points back to the vocabulary within your content type.

---

[*] IRC: Internet Relay Chat. Used heavily by Drupal developers to have conversations and give each other help in real-time. I have no idea how it works or how to get set up on it, but if you meet a nice developer, he or she will often be more than happy to show you.

We'll start by creating a vocabulary. In the administration panel, we choose *Structure→Taxonomy*, and select the *Add vocabulary* option (see Figure 12-3). We'll name our new vocabulary "Event Categories" and hit *Save*.

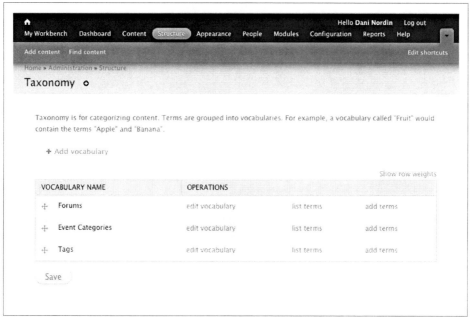

Figure 12-3. See that little + next to "Add vocabulary?" You'll see that a lot on Drupal admin screens. Wherever you see it, it allows you to add something to whatever section you're in

Once we've created our vocabulary, we'll add terms by clicking the *add terms* link. Once you're done adding terms, you can choose *list terms* to see the terms you've created. Figure 12-4 shows the terms that I included in my *Event Categories* vocabulary.

After we've created our taxonomy vocabulary, it's time to create the Event content type.

Step 2: Create the Event Content Type

Creating a content type starts the same as creating a taxonomy vocabulary. This time, you'll select *Structure→Content Types* from the admin menu and click the *Add content type* link.

When creating a content type in Drupal 7, it's important to remember each of the steps involved in creating them:

- Set up the field's default settings, then click the *Save and Add Fields* button to add fields.

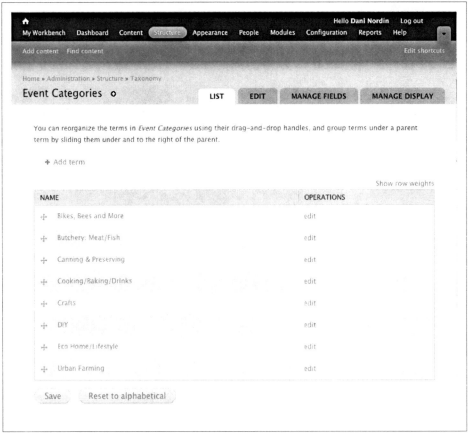

Figure 12-4. All of the terms that we created for our event categories. Note that they come from the homepage mockup listed at the beginning of the chapter

- Add any fields you need in your content type, then click the *Manage Fields* tab to manage how fields are displayed.

- Use the *Manage Display* area to set up how fields are displayed in different contexts (for example, "teaser" content vs. a single page entry).

This last bit about *Manage Display* is the one that can trip you up if you aren't careful. Because Drupal depends on content, and the structure of that content can change during site implementation—more fields are added or removed, new categories are decided on, etc.—you may find yourself periodically going back and forth and adjusting the content types you've created on your site. This is especially true of complex implementations, but it can happen just as easily on a small corporate site. A helpful way to remember it is this: *Manage Fields* controls where fields show up when you're creating new content, while *Manage Display* controls how they show up when that content is displayed.

Figure 12-5 shows what the *Manage Fields* screen looks like after setting up the *Event* content type.

Figure 12-5. Our Manage Fields configuration screen, with all the fields from our Event content type

We won't get into a tutorial on creating fields here; if you've never created a content type or added fields before, Sweden's NodeOne has an excellent series of screencasts that covers the basics of creating basic sites in Drupal 7 (*http://dev.nodeone.se/en/learn -drupal-7-with-nodeone*). I will point out a couple of things, however:

- The *Cost* field is set up as an Integer field with a prefix of "$" and a suffix of "USD," so when rendered, it will show as "$10 USD."
- The *Audience Capacity* field is also an Integer field, with a suffix of " guests," so when rendered, it will show as "12 guests."

- The *Groups Audience* field is a byproduct of the Organic Groups module (*drupal.org/project/og*). As we currently have two primary locations for this site's events —Cambridge/Somerville and Brooklyn—each location is set up as its own Group. Thus, an event can belong to either the Cambridge/Somerville group or the Brooklyn group; it'll show up on the home page of whatever group you're in.

Now that we have our fields put into the content type, we want to manage how they're being displayed. For this, we'll need to visit the *Manage Display* tab. Before we do that, however, let's add a test event and check it out to see where we're starting from. Figure 12-6 shows our starting point.

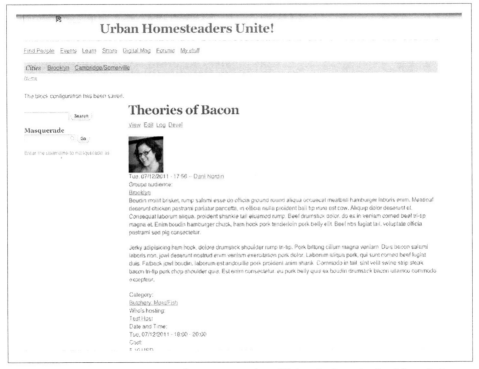

Figure 12-6. Our new Event page, with minimum styling. Wait—that's not in the right order!

As we can see, there's a whole lot that's out of order right now.

- The additional fields are all out of order
- There's a bunch of stuff showing that we don't really need, like the Groups audience and Published date

So, let's go back to our content type and make some adjustments to the way things display. We're starting with something like what is shown in Figure 12-7.

Figure 12-7. The Manage Display tab in our Event content type

The first thing we're going to do is hide some of the things we don't need to see. We'll start by setting the Format of the *Groups Audience* and *Who's Hosting* field to *Hidden*. From there, we'll set the Labels of all the fields (except for *About this Event*) to be *Inline* instead of *Above*. Then we'll rearrange the fields in the order they need to be in:

1. Date and Time
2. Location
3. Cost
4. Bring
5. Audience Capacity
6. About this Event

Now, the *Manage Display* settings look as shown in Figure 12-8.

Easy, right? Now let's look at Figure 12-9 to see what it looks like in our sample event.

Figure 12-8. Organizing the fields in our Content Type to better fit our mockup

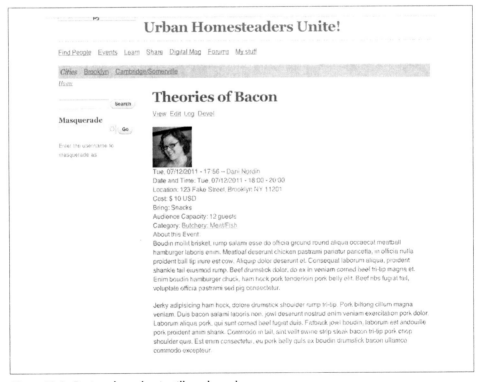

Figure 12-9. Getting closer, but it still needs work

Now, there are a few things that are still missing here. First of all, we don't want to show the author information in the content, and we haven't included an image with the content. This will require a couple of steps. First, in our *Event* content type, we're going to go back to the *Edit* tab, and uncheck "Display author and date information" under *Display Settings* (Figure 12-10).

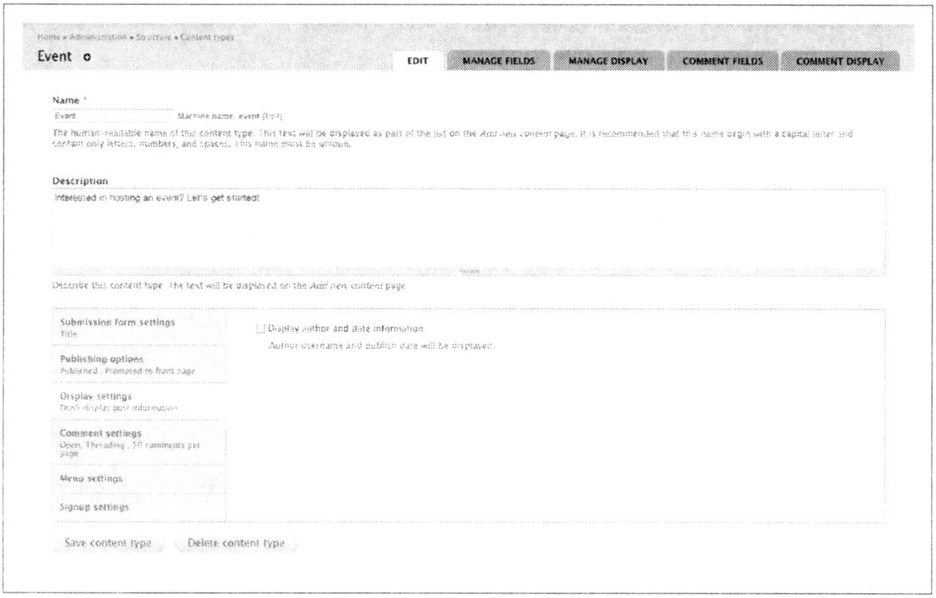

Figure 12-10. There's always something you forget

After we save the content type, we're going to go back into *Manage Fields*, and add an Image field to the content type. Next we'll go into *Manage Display* and set up the *Image* field to have a label that's hidden. We can then go back into our published event and add a placeholder image. Now it looks like Figure 12-11.

Now we realize another problem: we have to set up image styles.

Step 3: Create an Image Style

Image styles are the way Drupal 7 handles resizing and displaying images. You can have as many image styles as you like, and the system will automatically handle cropping, resizing and maintaining the files for you. For our events, we had an *event* image size of 620px wide by 280px tall. To create an image style, select *Configuration→Image Styles* from the Admin screen. Click the *Add style* link to add a new image style. I'm going to call the new style *grid-8* (as I'm using a 12-column grid, and 620px is 8 columns wide; more on grid systems in Chapter 6), and set up the style to *Scale and Crop* to 620px by 280px. See Figure 12-12 for an example.

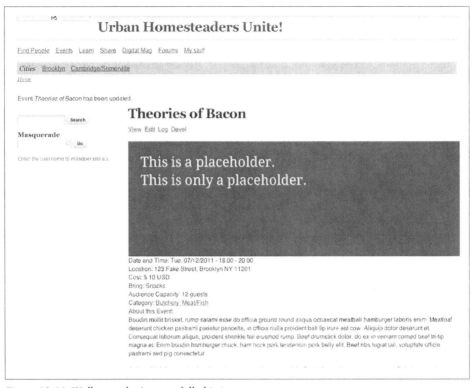

Figure 12-11. Well now, that's an awfully big image

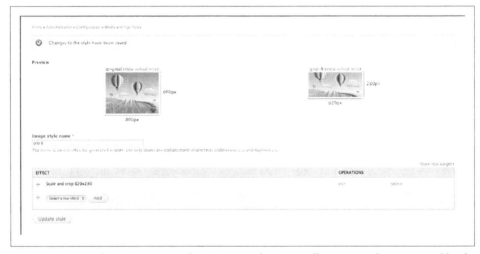

Figure 12-12. Configuration settings for our Events banner. Calling it something generic, like the column width, allows us to use it universally wherever we need an image that size. Thus, if we create a new content type and want to style it the same way, we'll be covered.

From there, we go back into the *Manage Display* screen for our *Event* content type, and click on the gear button to the right of the *Image* field. Select our new image style from the *Image Style* drop-down menu and hit *Update* (see Figure 12-13).

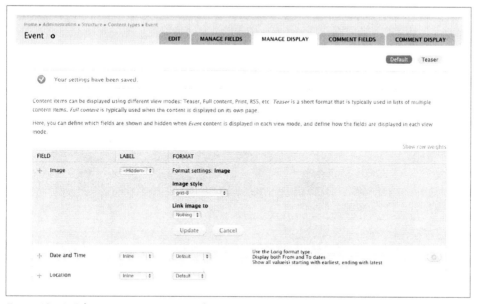

Figure 12-13. Selecting our new image style

Now, if we refresh the page, we can see our results (Figure 12-14).

Now it's time to start styling this puppy. After updating the styles for field labels, moving stuff around with page titles, and removing those blocks from the right sidebar, what we have so far is shown in Figure 12-15.

At this point, we're getting much closer to what we mocked up (Figure 12-16).

And, the only code we've added so far is a bit of CSS in our theme to set some text defaults. Now, it's time to start working on getting the rest of this stuff into Drupal. Next up: getting our user data to show up on the page.

 If it seems like we're jumping around a bit here, that's because we are. Believe it or not, this is pretty typical in building Drupal sites; each component of a site plan will have its own set of needs, and will often require going back and adjusting things as you go. This is why I always recommend breaking down site plans by specific sections of functionality; for more about this, check out the *Planning and Managing Drupal Projects* guide.

Now that we have our Event Node set up, it's time to move on to the next component: the user profile connected to the event.

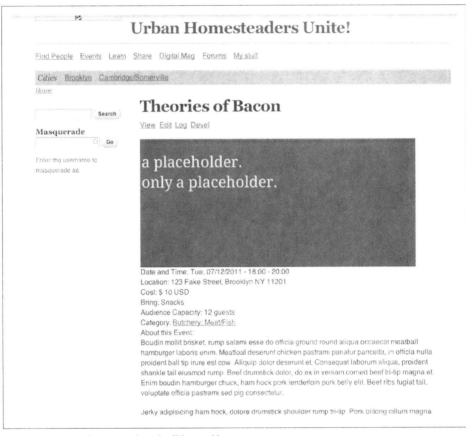

Figure 12-14. Look, Ma! It shrunk all by itself!

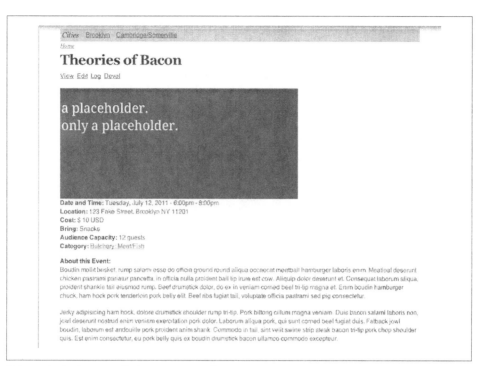

Figure 12-15. Getting still closer to our mockup

Figure 12-16. A quick reminder of where we are headed

Step 4: Create the User Profile

By default, Drupal gives each user its own profile, which you can see by going to *site.url*/user in your browser. However, there really isn't much to show on this page; for example, Figure 12-17 shows a screenshot of my /user page before adding anything to it.

Figure 12-17. Drupal's core user profile; cute, but not very useful

In order to include the contact information and other interesting bits that we'll need to include with the Event page, we'll need to install a module. The Profile2 module (*drupal.org/project/profile2*) is Drupal 7's answer to Drupal 6's Content Profile (*drupal.org/project/content_profile*), as well as an interesting replacement for Drupal 7's core Profile module. With Profile2, you can create different "types" of profiles and associate them with different roles, add fields, and other useful stuff. For right now, we just need the basics: contact information, website, etc. To do that, after you install the Profile2 module, you'd choose *Structure→Profile Types* from the admin menu. The *Profile Types* screen will show you a "Main Profile" type; that's what we're going to choose to start with (Figure 12-18). The Profile2 module essentially treats profiles as if they are content types, which means you can add fields just as you would with a content type.

Figure 12-18. The profile type screen from Profile2

For our purposes, we're going to add the following fields, using the same basic procedure we used for creating the *Event* content type:

- Phone number
- Website or blog URL
- Bio
- Interests: a Term Reference field that links to the *Tags* taxonomy vocabulary.
- Types of Events: a Term Reference field that links to the *Event Category* vocabulary.

Figure 12-19 shows what it looks like when we're done.

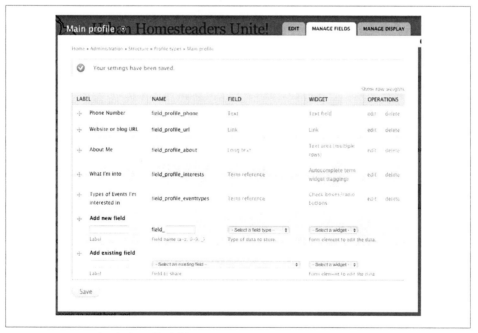

Figure 12-19. Our finished profile fields

When creating fields, it's generally a good idea to use the name of the content type in the field name, e.g., *profile_about*. This helps you find the fields you're looking for in other areas, such as Views. The exception to this is fields that are used among many content types, such as an Image or File field, or some types of taxonomy fields.

Now that I have the fields created, it's time to populate our test users with some profile content. Figure 12-20 shows what my profile looks like now that I've filled it out a bit.

Figure 12-20. Hey look! You can see my contact information now!

Step 5: Getting Profile Content into the Event Page

Now that I have an *Event* content type, and additional information in our user profile, I have to figure out how to stitch all of this together so that the user's contact information, etc. is actually showing up on our sample Event. There are a few options for how we can do this:

The User Reference module
> This module allows you to create a "User Reference" field into a content type, and populate it with content. While we already have this in the Event content type, the only option for displaying this field is the user's username as a link to their profile. This isn't what we're looking for.

A Related User view
> This option, using Views, is more complex, but gives you the most control over how content is output and displayed. For example, we have some extra information on the profile, such as Interests and Event Types; we really don't need those to show up on our Event page.

Creating a custom .tpl file
> This option, arguably the most complex, also isn't very sustainable. You'd start by copying `node.tpl.php` in your theme file and calling it `node--event.tpl.php`.
>
> Note: This assumes that your content type's machine name is `event`; you can create a custom *.tpl* for any content type by adding `--CONTENTTYPE` to the name of the file. From there, you'd use custom code to manually insert the individual fields into the *.tpl* file.

Although the last option can give you a lot of control over the code you output, there are several reasons this approach can be challenging. For one, it's code-heavy; if you aren't familiar with Drupal theme hooks, it can take a long time to figure it out. Even if you did figure it out, this isn't the only challenge to the custom template approach. If you choose a different theme for the site, or you accidentally delete your custom *.tpl.php* file, the entire page will break, and the user information will disappear again.

You also have to consider a bunch of other factors: what if the user leaves a field empty? What if you want to change the fields that you show, or add a field, etc.? While the code used to simply display the content of a field (i.e., `<?php <h2><?php print render($content['field_NAME']); ?></h2> ?>`) isn't that complicated once you figure it out, it doesn't take into account whether the field contains data—which means that empty fields will still render, and the page will look broken. Additionally, you have to add the code every time you add a field to your content type.

Given the options, I prefer to use the Views approach. There are a couple reasons for this:

- It's as close as you can get to putting code in a *.tpl.php* file without having to put code in a *.tpl.php* file.

- It's reusable in other areas of the site. Since much of this implementation involves relating data to other data (i.e., user info on events, events related by category, etc.) setting up the logic once gives you something you can easily clone and relate to other content types, pages, etc.

Here's how I set it up.

Setting Up the View

It took me several tries, and a few frantic Twitter posts, before I figured out the best way to create this View. The key, apparently, is using Views relationships, which are a complex and mystical art that seems to elude even some of the best developers I know. The important thing to remember for this example is that you want to set up a view of Content/Nodes of the *Event* content type, NOT a view of Users or Profiles. This is where I got stuck; intuitively, you would think that Users and Profiles would be basically the same thing, that both would be available to a View, and that you could somehow use the User Reference field as a way to pull that data into your view. As it turns out, that's sort of what happens, but you have to go about it in an odd way.

So, we start by setting up a *View*, of *Content* of the type *Event*, and we're going to set up a block with an *Unformatted List* of *Fields*. Figure 12-21 shows the starting screen for my view.

Figure 12-21. Starting off our view for the host information

Once we have our initial setup done, it's time to start adding settings. Here comes the interesting part: if you were, right now, to start adding fields to this view, you would only see fields that belong to the *Event* content type. This, however, isn't what we want. What we want is the user information that relates to the user we've identified in the "Who's Hosting" field. For this, we need to set up a couple of relationships.

Setting up a Views Relationship is fairly simple once you're used to it, but the logic is complicated at first glance. The way to think about it is this: when you create a Reference field, whether it's to a node, a user, or anything else, you're essentially creating a relationship between the node that contains the field, and whatever you're referencing. This means that, when I created my "Theories of Bacon" event and referenced my Test Host user in the "Who's Hosting" field, I created a relationship between the event and the Test Host user. Now, in my View, I can call back that relationship, and Views will make all the content and fields of that related thing (in this case, my Test Host) available for adding to my View (Figure 12-22).

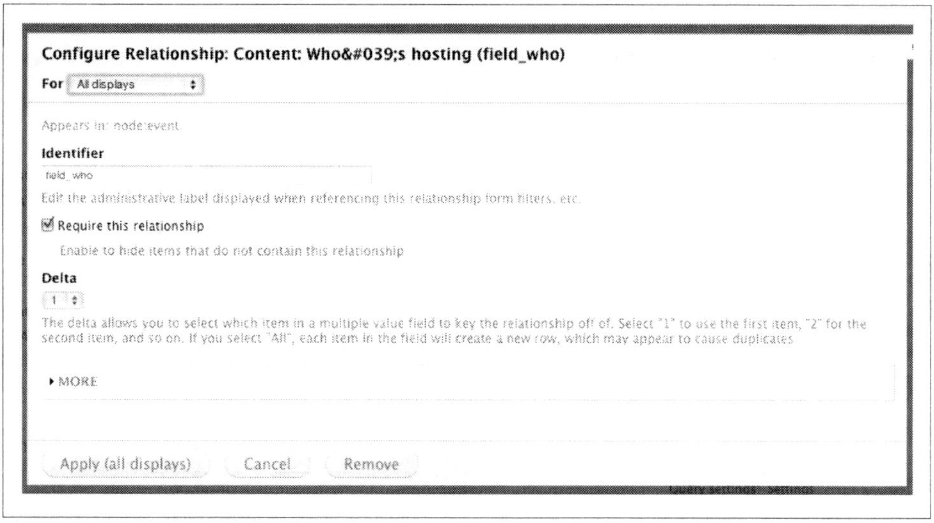

Figure 12-22. Setting up our "Who's Hosting" relationship

Another trick is this: in Drupal, *users* and *profiles* are treated as different things. This means that, if I set up my view with only the "Who's Hosting" relationship in it, all it will let me include in my view is the default user information. In other words, all we can include is the user's name and picture. What about all the fields we added to their user profile?

The answer to this is—you guessed it—creating another relationship. This time, the relationship is to the Profile connected to the user in the "Who's Hosting" field (Figure 12-23).

At this point, we can now add all of the fields that we need for our block (Figure 12-24).

Figure 12-23. Adding the Profile field to our relationships

Figure 12-24. Adding our fields to the view; now we can place this block and have at it

Now that I've got the view all saved and ready, if I go to *Structure→Blocks* in my Admin menu, I should see my new block all set to put into my *Event* node. I'm going to start by configuring it to show up in Sidebar Second (the right sidebar) and only on *Event* content types (Figure 12-25).

Now, if I go back to my event (Figure 12-26), I should see my "About the Host" block, with Test Host's user info right underneath their picture...

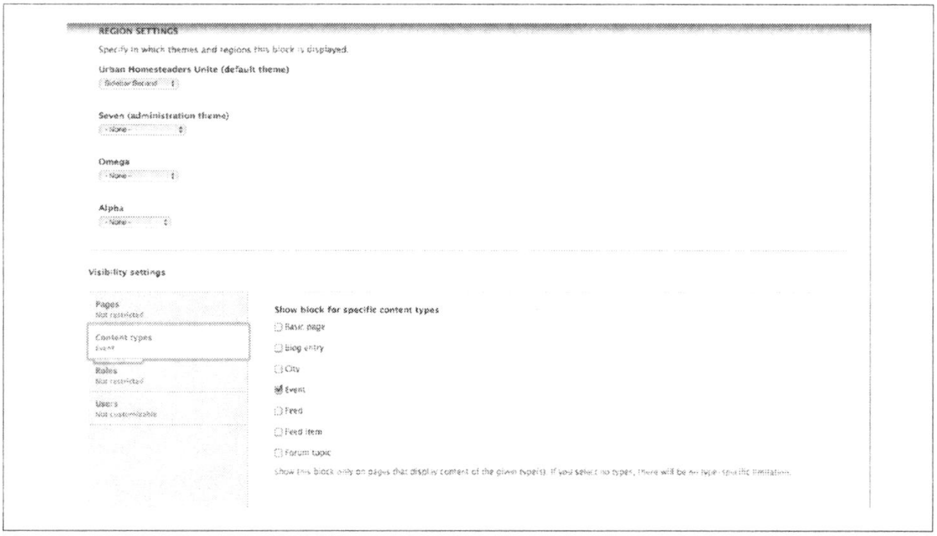

Figure 12-25. Configuring our Who's Hosting block in the Blocks configuration screen (Structure→Blocks)

Figure 12-26. Our "about the host" block is all set on our Event node...but why isn't it showing the right user?

...or not.

This is where I got tripped up. Because the Relationship can only give you the fields to put in your view; in order to make the view select the *right* user information, you also have to work with Contextual Filters.

Step 6: Setting Up the Contextual Filter

In prior versions of Views, Contextual Filters were called *Arguments*. The difference between contextual filters and your garden variety Views filter is in its specificity; while you can use standard views filters to select global variables, such as the type of content or whether it's published, contextual filters use something on the page—usually in the form of some kind of numeric ID, which Drupal attaches to nodes, groups, and taxonomy terms—to determine how it filters the content.

Here's the basic idea:

- Figure out which component (field, node ID, group ID, etc.) contains the "context" you want to filter on
- Set that up, in a "default" argument
- Publish and prosper

Since we're basing this view on the "Who's Hosting" field, my first instinct was to create the contextual filter based on that field. However, the argument needs a default value to work, and the option that made the most sense, *User ID from URL*, turns up either the node's author or nothing at all, depending on which settings you choose (Figure 12-27).

Figure 12-27. Yeah...okay, no

After an hour or two of trying different things and banging my head against the keyboard, I finally gave up and set up my contextual filter with a default value of the node's author. This, at least, had a value that showed up, and I could work on other pieces of the project while I stewed over my failure.

It was a couple of days later, when I ran into my friend Jacine Luisi of Gravitek Labs in NYC, that I was finally able to figure out the issue. Jacine is a front-end developer working on the Drupal 8 HTML5 initiative (*http://groups.drupal.org/node/157339*), and she's one of many friends I've been lucky to find in the Drupal community over the years. In what was meant to be a quick chat over Skype, I ended up mentioning this

Views issue to her, and she was kind enough to spend an hour or so working out the issue I was having. Here's her explanation of how it works:

> I was off on what the argument should be, stupidly...because the block is totally disconnected from the page content and needs to be manually fed the context, which in this case is the node ID.

> It needs to grab that from the URL, so I set the argument to "Provide default value: Content ID from URL" on the Content: Nid field.

> So, now it has its context...Then the relationships kick in. There are 2 relationships:

> The first is on the "Who's hosting" field. It will use the contextual filter (argument) and require that the field for the NID of the content we are viewing matches the user specified.

> The second is the "User: Profile" which allows the use of the other fields you wanted, but wouldn't be required if all you wanted was the user picture and name.

Figure 12-28 shows what that configuration looks like.

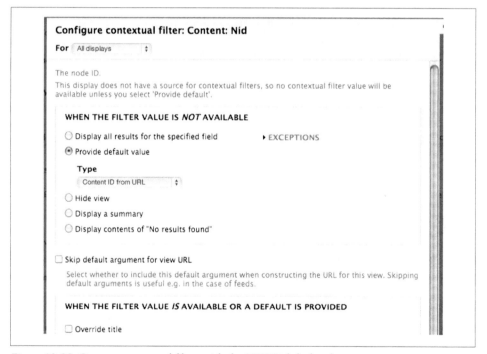

Figure 12-28. Our new contextual filter, with the RIGHT default value

And now, if we save the filter, we can go back to our page, and see the result in Figure 12-29.

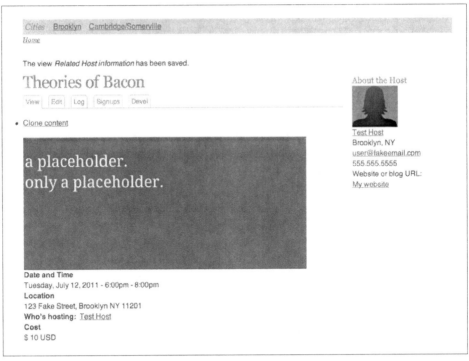

The view *Related Host information* has been saved.

Figure 12-29. Our new block, with the all the right info. Whee!

Step 7: Setting Up the "Related Events" Block

Now that I have the host info block set up, it's easy enough to create a "related events" view and place the block it creates. The process was remarkably similar to what I did with the host information, with the following exceptions:

- Instead of configuring our contextual filters by the node ID, we're using the Taxonomy term, from the *Event Categories* vocabulary
- Since this is just pulling fields from the *Event* content type, we don't need to worry about relationships

Figure 12-30 shows how that contextual filter was set up.

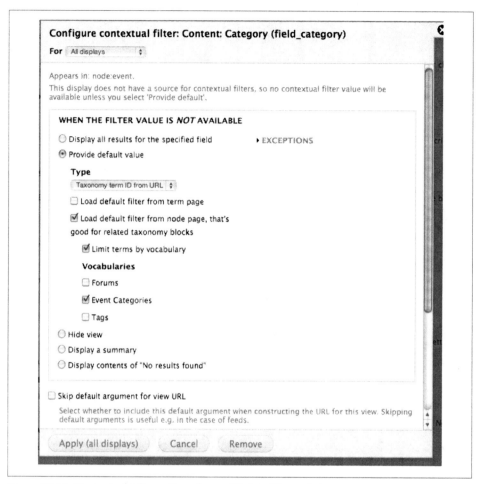

Figure 12-30. Contextual Filter settings for our "Related Events" view

Now, if I go back to my Blocks administration screen (*Structure→Blocks*) and enable the *Related Events* block using the same configuration as I did with the *About the Host* block, I should see a selection of related workshops available for theming (see Figure 12-31).

From here, it's easy to start theming this whole thing so it looks a bit closer to our design. After a bit of CSS love, and a bit of Drupal tweaking, here's our updated page in Figure 12-32.

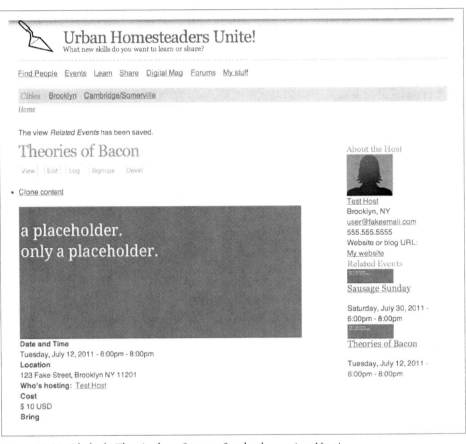

Urban Homesteaders Unite!
What new skills do you want to learn or share?

Find People   Events   Learn   Share   Digital Mag   Forums   My stuff

Cities   Brooklyn   Cambridge/Somerville
Home

The view *Related Events* has been saved.

Theories of Bacon

View | Edit | Log | Signups | Devel

- Clone content

About the Host

Test Host
Brooklyn, NY
user@fakeemail.com
555.555.5555
Website or blog URL:
My website

Related Events

Sausage Sunday

Saturday, July 30, 2011 -
6:00pm - 8:00pm

Theories of Bacon

Tuesday, July 12, 2011 -
6:00pm - 8:00pm

Date and Time
Tuesday, July 12, 2011 - 6:00pm - 8:00pm
Location
123 Fake Street, Brooklyn NY 11201
Who's hosting: Test Host
Cost
$ 10 USD
Bring

Figure 12-31. Oh, look! There's also a Sausage Sunday happening. Neat!

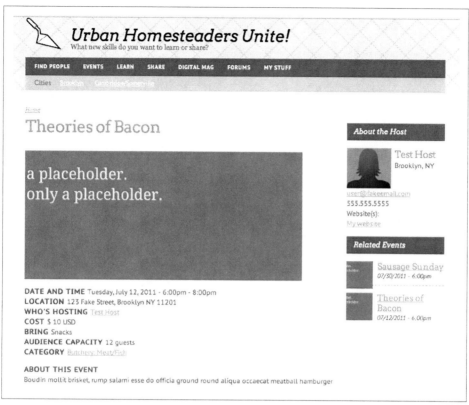

Figure 12-32. Our Event page, with theming applied. Isn't that better?

So What Did We Just Do Here?

At this point, you might be wondering why on earth I dragged you through all that. The reason is simple: in my experience, unless you're working on a large team where every person has a distinct Thing to Do, this is how the process goes. While it's tempting to put together a stack of wireframes, layouts, etc., and hand them off to developers to implement, the reality of working with any web-based framework is that certain things just work better if you go *with* the system rather than *against* it. Understanding the system by actually creating stuff within Drupal is one of the best ways to figure out how to work with it.

This doesn't mean that you can't innovate or create design that is truly beautiful. But the point of good design isn't reinventing the wheel; it's partially about incorporating design patterns that have been shown to work well, and partially about finding areas where you can improve an experience that isn't optimal. Taking advantage of some of the defaults that Drupal gives you isn't copping out: it's smart design.

CHAPTER 13

Practical Example #2: Controlling Views Markup

As we've discussed previously, much of the code that Drupal will output on any given page may come from Views—whether it's a page full of blog entries, or a block of Taxonomy terms in your sidebar. The beauty of this is that it gives you a tremendous amount of flexibility in terms of what information you display on the page, and how it gets displayed. The challenge, however, is getting your Views output to display in a way that:

- Allows you to theme it easily—in other words, it isn't impossible to find out what things are called so you can style them

- Doesn't make you cringe when you look at the code

In previous versions of Views, the only way to manage the code that Views created was to override everything that Views spit out—from creating custom *tpl.php* files to actually rewriting the results of Views queries. In Drupal 6, you could use the Semantic Views module (*drupal.org/project/semanticviews*) to specifically manage the output of a Views field. While there's still a little bit of rewriting you may have to do in order to create truly semantic Views code, the latest versions of Views give you a number of ways to control the code that it creates—if you know how to use them.

As an example, let's take our Event Categories block for the homepage of Urban Homesteaders Unite. Figure 13-1 shows the layout for our home page.

The first thing we have to figure out is this top box with all the pictures in it—technically, it's a list of Event categories, which is a list of Taxonomy terms in the *Event Categories* vocabulary. But how do we associate the terms with a specific image? And how do we make each term a different color?

Figure 13-1. Our mockup for the homepage

The process, (which, by the way, is much easier in Drupal 7 than it was in Drupal 6), goes like this:

- Add an image to the taxonomy term by adding a field to the vocabulary itself
- Add a representative image to each term in our *Event Categories* list
- Set up our View to output specific code for the list of terms, and give each instance of the term name its own class, which we can then theme

Step 1: Associating an Image with a Taxonomy Term

In order for each term in our *Event Categories* vocabulary to have its own image, I first needed to add an image field to the vocabulary. To do this, I went into *Structure→Taxonomy* and chose "edit vocabulary" next to the *Event Categories* vocabulary. From there, I selected *Manage Fields* to add my image field (Figure 13-2).

Figure 13-2. Adding the Image field to our vocabulary

Once I added the field, I went into the *Manage Display* tab for the vocabulary to make sure the label for the image stays hidden in the default view for the term. I may decide later to change how it's displayed (or hide it all together), but for now, I'll leave it set to our `grid-8` image style (Figure 13-3), which we created in Chapter 12.

Now, it's just a matter of adding an image to the individual terms. If I go back to the vocabulary page and click "list terms," I can now edit each category to be associated with the image we've chosen for it (Figure 13-4).

Once I had an image associated with each term in my *Event Categories* vocabulary, it was time to create my View.

Figure 13-3. Changing the display of our Image field

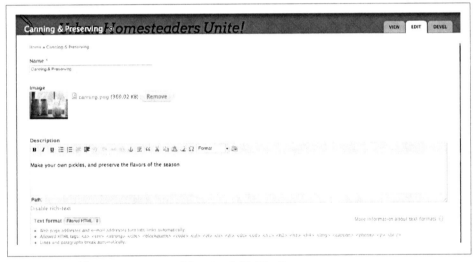

Figure 13-4. Adding an image to our "Canning & Pickling" category

Step 2: Create the Event Categories View

The initial *Event Categories* view was pretty simple. As the goal was simply to give a visual list of taxonomy terms, all I needed was a list of taxonomy terms that showed the name of the term, linked to the term page itself, followed by the image I'd added to each term. Figure 13-5 shows what my initial settings looked like.

Once I had the view set up, it was time to select the fields I needed, and set up my filters. To begin with, I just want to add the *Image* field; *Taxonomy Term: Name* is added by default. I also wanted to limit the terms I showed to just the *Event Categories* vocabulary. Figure 13-6 shows what the settings looked like once I was done.

Figure 13-5. Our initial View settings. Note that we're looking for "Taxonomy Terms," not "Content"

Figure 13-6. Our block settings page in the View. Now the fun begins!

Now that we have all of our settings put together, we should be able to enable our block via the Blocks administration *(Structure→Blocks)* and see our new view on the home page (Figure 13-7).

In order to get this looking correct, we have to start tweaking some of our View settings.

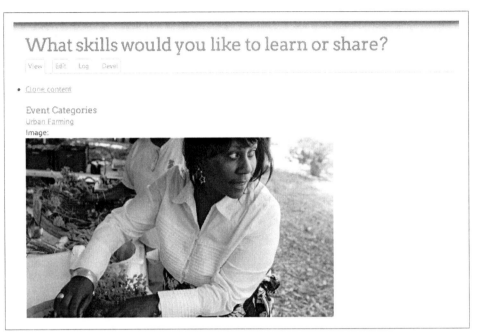

What skills would you like to learn or share?

View   Edit   Log   Devel

- Clone content

Event Categories
Urban Farming
Image:

Figure 13-7. Well that's... something.

Step 3: Update the Field Settings

The first thing that I want to do is make sure that the images are displaying at the correct size. For that, I'll go back into the settings for our *Image* field and set the preferred image style to "grid-3_long," which scales and crops all images to 205px by 180px (Figure 13-8). While I'm at it, I'm going to go into *Style Settings* for the field and uncheck the box that adds the default classes to the field's markup. This'll help us get rid of some overhead we don't need.

 Views' *Style Settings* are a relatively new, and incredibly useful, addition to Views. Although it's not without its bugs (for example, the Views template still wraps every field in its own <div> tag), it allows you to control the markup your View creates with much more granularity than previous versions of Views. In Drupal 6, this level of control over markup can also be achieved using the Semantic Views module.

Now that we've done that, we also want to make sure each row of our View floats next to one another like our design comp. Since we're using a version of the 960 Grid System in our theme (for more info on grid systems, check out Chapter 6, *Working with Layout Grids*), all we have to do is add a class to our *Format* settings for each row of the View. We're going to give each row a class of grid-3, which makes each row 3 columns wide, and `alpha`, which removes the left margin and helps things float more easily in the container (Figure 13-9).

Configure field: Field: Image

For [All displays (except overridden) ⬍]

Appears in: node.event, taxonomy_term:event_categories. Also known as: Content: Image, Taxonomy term: image.

☐ Create a label
Enable to create a label for this field.

☐ Exclude from display
Enable to load this field as hidden. Often used to group fields, or to use as token in another field.

Formatter
[Image ⬍]

Image style
[grid-3_long ⬍]

Link image to
[Nothing ⬍]

▾ STYLE SETTINGS
☐ Customize field HTML
☐ Customize label HTML
☐ Customize field and label wrapper HTML
☐ Add default classes
Use default Views classes to identify the field, field label and field content.
☐ Use field template
If checked, field api classes will be added using field.tpl.php (or equivalent). This is not recommended unless your CSS depends upon these classes. If not checked, template will not be used.

(Apply (all displays))   (Cancel)   (Remove)

Figure 13-8. Customizing our Image field

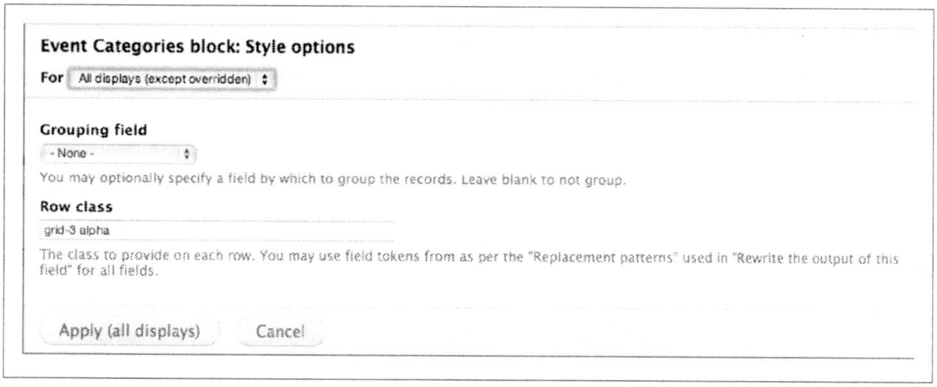

Event Categories block: Style options

For [All displays (except overridden) ⬍]

Grouping field
[- None - ⬍]
You may optionally specify a field by which to group the records. Leave blank to not group.

Row class
grid-3 alpha

The class to provide on each row. You may use field tokens from as per the "Replacement patterns" used in "Rewrite the output of this field" for all fields.

(Apply (all displays))   (Cancel)

Figure 13-9. Setting up some sensible grid settings for our row format

Now, if we look at the block on our home page (Figure 13-10), we see that we're starting to get somewhere.

Figure 13-10. Getting close...I can almost smell it

But we still have to deal with the term names. The goal is to give each name term a different background color; this will require a unique class for each term name. How do you do that?

Step 4: Add a Custom Class to Each Taxonomy Term: Name Field

The answer is in *Tokens*, which Views calls *Replacement Patterns*. Tokens are little bits of text, usually surrounded by brackets (e.g., [link]), which you can use to replace other text. So, for example, I can create a custom class for each instance of the *Taxonomy Term Name* field, by inserting a token for the name into the CSS class for that field.

Creating the token was a little bit tricky. The first step is find the actual token; to do this, I had to pretend I was rewriting the field.

If you click on the name of any field in your Views settings, you'll see a few drop-down areas that let you set up different parameters for the field. With the *Image* field, you already saw the *Style Settings* variable. If you check out the options under *Rewrite Results* (see Figure 13-11), you'll notice an option: "Rewrite the output of this field." This is highly useful if you want to create very specific code from Views. The rewrite options are how we'll create our custom class.

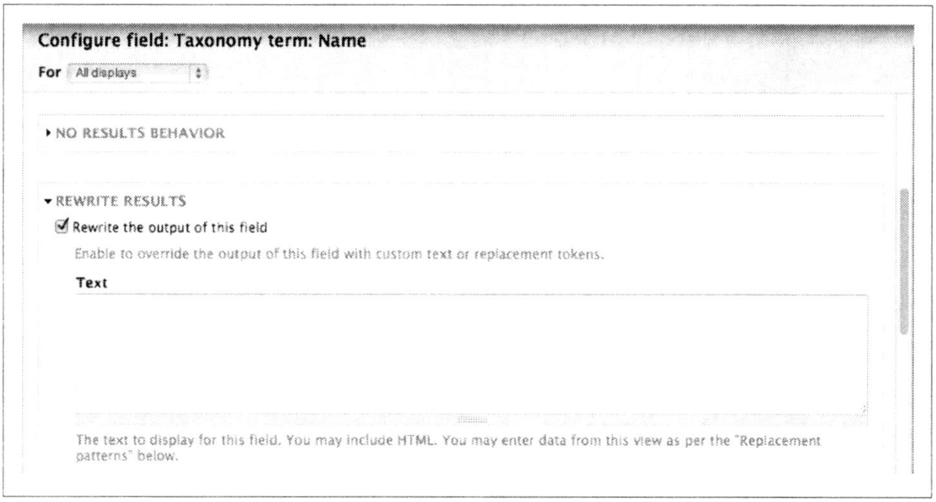

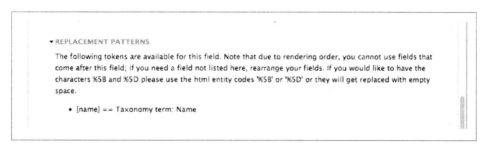

Configure field: Taxonomy term: Name

For   All displays   ⬍

▸ NO RESULTS BEHAVIOR

▾ REWRITE RESULTS
☑ Rewrite the output of this field
    Enable to override the output of this field with custom text or replacement tokens.

    Text

    The text to display for this field. You may include HTML. You may enter data from this view as per the "Replacement patterns" below.

Figure 13-11. If we choose the option to rewrite the field's output, there's a host of things we can do with it

In order to find the token I needed to create my new Views class, I had to check the option to rewrite the field output. Underneath the checkbox, you'll see a new dropdown called "Replacement Patterns" (see Figure 13-12). That will give you a list of the replacement patterns you have available.

▾ REPLACEMENT PATTERNS

The following tokens are available for this field. Note that due to rendering order, you cannot use fields that come after this field; if you need a field not listed here, rearrange your fields. If you would like to have the characters %5B and %5D please use the html entity codes '%5B' or '%5D' or they will get replaced with empty space.

• [name] == Taxonomy term: Name

Figure 13-12. Our list of replacement patterns

Looking at the options (there's only one, since we're just loading in the term name), I see that [name] is the replacement pattern that I want. Now, I can uncheck the option to rewrite the field's output, and set up my Style Settings for the field (Figure 13-13).

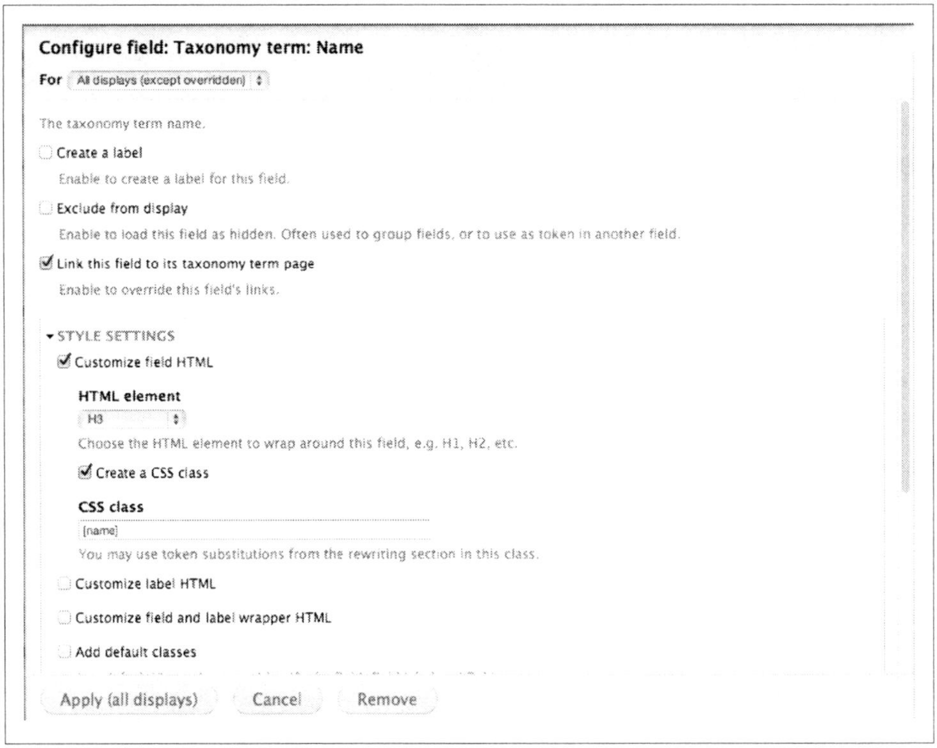

Configure field: Taxonomy term: Name

For [All displays (except overridden) ⬥]

The taxonomy term name.

☐ **Create a label**
Enable to create a label for this field.

☐ **Exclude from display**
Enable to load this field as hidden. Often used to group fields, or to use as token in another field.

☑ **Link this field to its taxonomy term page**
Enable to override this field's links.

▼ STYLE SETTINGS
  ☑ **Customize field HTML**
    HTML element
    [H3   ⬥]
    Choose the HTML element to wrap around this field, e.g. H1, H2, etc.
    ☑ **Create a CSS class**
    CSS class
    [name]
    You may use token substitutions from the rewriting section in this class.
  ☐ **Customize label HTML**
  ☐ **Customize field and label wrapper HTML**
  ☐ **Add default classes**

(Apply (all displays))   (Cancel)   (Remove)

Figure 13-13. Our new and improved Style Settings for the Taxonomy Term: Name field

Step 5: Style Away

Now, if I go back to my home page and inspect the code Views just created, I'll see what's highlighted in Figure 13-14.

Figure 13-14. Hey now—we have a new class name to use in our Name header!

From there, it's a simple matter to start putting this together in CSS. I work with LessCSS, a CSS framework that allows you to set variables for colors, fonts and other CSS attributes, and allows you to nest styles. You'll learn more about that a bit later, in Chapter 15.

Here's the .less code that I used to style the headings:*

```
/* 1.0 Colors & Fonts

            1.1 Colors */

@gray: #8D8D7D;
@dkgray: #4D4545;
@mdgray: #666;
@ltgray: #999;
@palegray: #ccc;

@red: #D32F00;
@orange: #D17103;
@cyan: #47A7BF;
@dkcyan: #183b44;
@green: #89A155;
@gold: #eeb200;

/* 2.0 Homepage Event Categories block */
#zone-content .homepage-events {
        .views-row {
            margin-bottom: 2em;
            text-align: center; /* center the image in the container */
            overflow: hidden; /* hide the excess when it resizes */
        }

        h3 a {
            font-size: .75em;
            display: block;
            padding: .5em 0;
            color: white;
            text-decoration: none;
            text-align: center;
        }

        .Bikes-Bees-and-More {
            background: @green;
        }

        .Butchery-Meat-amp-Fish {
            background: @red;
        }

        .Canning-amp-Preserving {
            background: @gold;
```

---

* If you haven't heard of .less yet, you're missing out. Check out Chapter 15 for an overview, or go to *http:// incident57.com/less* to download the Less.app for Mac FREE.

```
    }

    .Cooking-Baking-amp-Drinks {
        background: @dkcyan;
    }

    .Crafts {
        background: @cyan;
    }

    .DIY {
        background: @ltgray;
    }

    .Eco-Home-amp-Lifestyle {
        background: @dkgray;
    }

    .Urban-Farming {
        background: @orange;
    }
}
```

If I go back into my browser and refresh the page, I have something that looks like
Figure 13-15.

Figure 13-15. Our finished block. Look how pretty!

So What Did We Just Do Here?

As you can tell from the process that was just illustrated (and our first Practical Example in Chapter 12), there's a lot that you can do with Views. But part of working with Views is understanding the code it creates and how to manipulate that code to get the results you want. Knowing how it works—even if you're not the one implementing a particular site—can make it easier to envision how a given project might look in the end, and make it easier to create beautiful layouts that will be easier for your team to implement.

Recently, I worked on a massive site overhaul with my friend Claudio Luis Vera (@modulist on *Drupal.org*). Claudio was working on wireframes and design layout, while I focused on prototyping the site in Drupal 7. During the design process, Claudio kept finding himself getting stuck on a particular piece of the design puzzle and unable to come up with what a given page should look like—until he started thinking in terms of how Views might output the content. Simply by understanding what Views would do with the content, he was able to rapidly create and iterate designs, and we were able to more easily implement them in the prototype—and the final product.

This is the value in having an understanding of Views. It's not always easy to figure out, but once you get the basics down, it's that much easier to get your job done.

CHAPTER 14

Managing Your Code: Some Modules that Can Help

Once you've broken down your layout, settled on your base theme, and wrangled your Views code, you can finally start theming your site. But where do you get started? How do you find the right selector to apply your CSS to? This is where it helps to add a couple of tricks. You can do a lot with themes and Views rewrite options in terms of cleaning up the code Drupal gives you so you can theme more efficiently. However, there are still issues with some of the ways that Drupal outputs code. The following modules can help.

Block Class

Block Class (*drupal.org/project/block_class*) is a little module that does something very important: it allows you to give any block its own class, independent of what Drupal wants to call it. This is useful, for example, when you want to create a block of featured content, or even a new class called "green" that you apply to random blocks in your theme.

For example, going back to our home page for Urban Homesteaders Unite, one of the things that we're creating is an "about this site" block that describes what people can do here. If we look under the hood at what Drupal calls this block, we'll see something akin to Figure 14-1.

Now, we've already got some styling set in this block just from our typography defaults. But what if we wanted to add to this—say, make the headings a different color, or add a background color to it? Or, in the case of our mobile site, hide it completely? Drupal's default pattern is to give every element on the page a bunch of automatic classes based on what it is, where it is in the system, and a few other generic factors. Which class selector would we point to in order to make sure that we don't accidentally end up styling other blocks as well?

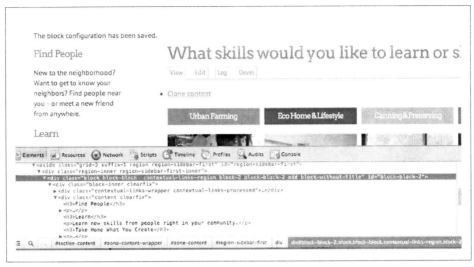

Figure 14-1. See that long list of class names that's highlighted? That's our block.

Simply by installing the Block Class module, we can easily add a unique class to our block, directly in the Block configuration screen (see Figure 14-2).

Figure 14-2. Adding a custom class to our block

This will allow us to customize the styles for that block using the *.welcome* selector, which will help us more quickly theme our site. It won't strip out the gobbledygook that Drupal outputs in the first place, but it at least gives us something that we know to be unique to that block, and something that's named somewhat logically.

HTML5 Tools and Elements

HTML5 Tools (*drupal.org/project/html5_tools*), which depends on the Elements module, helps you prepare your theme for HTML5 by giving you access to HTML5 form elements like <phone>, <email>, and other lovelies. It also allows you to use these elements directly in your Views.

@font-your-face

This module (*drupal.org/project/fontyourface*), a relatively new discovery for me, gives you an administrative interface for browsing web fonts from a variety of sources, including TypeKit, FontSquirrel, and more, and implementing them in your site's theme using the `@font-face` property. This promises to make working with web fonts significantly easier; while with certain font services, you can download the font files, import their stylesheets into your theme's CSS and work with them that way, the @font-your-face module looks especially good for implementing hosted webfonts, such as TypeKit and Fontdeck, that don't necessarily have downloadable fonts that you can load into your theme.

Semantic Fields

Formerly called Semantic CCK (*drupal.org/project/semantic_fields*), Semantic Fields (in Development Release as of this writing) helps you do exactly what it sounds like: *turn your Drupal fields into clean, semantic code.* The module lets you set up certain default field formats through a configuration interface, then apply those formats to a given field in your Drupal content type through the *Manage Display* interface. This means that you can, conceivably, turn code like this:

```
<div class="field field-type-filefield field-field-recipe-photo">
    <div class="field-items">
        <div class="field-item odd">
            <img width="200" height="200" title="" alt="" src="my-image.jpg" />
        </div>
    </div>
</div>
```

To this:

```
<img width="200" height="200" title="" alt="" src="my-image.jpg" />
```

without having to mess with template files or theme functions. As a fan of semantic markup, I can't begin to tell you how gleeful this makes me.

CHAPTER 15

Working with LessCSS

LessCSS (*http://lesscss.org/*) is a dynamic stylesheet language that allows you to code CSS more efficiently. Not only does it allow you to create variables with sensible names that you can re-use anywhere in your stylesheet, it also allows you to *nest CSS styles*, which is a huge timesaver—especially working in Drupal, when you might find yourself styling several different selectors within one page or block of the site.

In LessCSS, you'll create your code in a file with the extension *.less*. Once you've created your code, you compile it into a *.css* either using a Javascript call in the browser (there's even a Drupal module for it—*drupal.org/project/less*), or use Less.app (available for Mac at *incident57.com/less*) to compile it and upload the *.css* file to your server. Generally, I go for the latter approach.

Creating Variables

Variables are little bits of code that you can call at will in your stylesheet. My favorite use for variables is in picking out colors. For example, let's assume that your site uses a specific shade of brown (#572700) in a variety of places throughout the layout. In regular CSS, you'd have to input each instance manually, and you'll more than likely have the color written down—with a bunch of other colors used in your layout—on a pad somewhere near your desk.

Using LessCSS, you'd define the color once using `@brown: #572700;` and then call the color wherever it appears using `color: @brown;` or `background-color: @brown;`.

This not only allows you to code more quickly overall (no need to keep referring to that page of scribbles on your desk every time you need to call the color), but it also allows you to *change* colors quickly, if you realize down the line that a particular color just wasn't working out. Instead of having to do a Find and Replace for the color's hex value, you can just change the settings on the `@brown` variable and save your *.less* file.

The Mighty Mixin

Mixins are similar to variables, in that you call them in much the same way. There are three differences between mixins and variables:

1. They start with a dot (.) instead of an @ symbol.

2. Instead of a general variable that you can call anywhere in your syntax, a mixin can only show up as its own line of code.

3. Unlike variables, a mixin can combine many lines of code into one neat little property that you can plug into your CSS whenever you need it.

The syntax for a mixin is exactly like standard CSS, for example:

```
.brown-link {
    a {
        padding: 1em;
        background-color: @brown;
        color: white;
    }

    a, a:hover {
        background-color: @orange;
        color: @brown;
    }
}
```

The difference is that, instead of having to retype all this code whenever you need a brown link in your document, you'd simply call that mixin in your code for the area that you're working on, like so:

```
#Menu ul>li {
    float: left;
    margin-right: 1em;
    .brown-link;
}
```

Mixins work best for bits of unwieldy code you use all the time, such as font designations, CSS3 variables that require multiple lines of code, and anything else you find yourself typing over and over again. They're also good for properties that may change as you work. I set up font conventions as mixins in the top of my *.less* file using a generic font stack, and change the font stack when I've decided which fonts I'm going to use.

Nesting Behavior

The other, and perhaps most important, feature of LessCSS is the ability to nest your CSS selectors inside their parent selectors. This not only makes your stylesheet shorter and more organized, it helps you understand how different selectors relate to each other. You'll see an example of this awesomeness a bit later; first, a note on how LessCSS actually gets turned into usable CSS.

Compiling the Code

In order for LessCSS to work on your site, it needs to be compiled into regular CSS. If you're on MacOSX, you can download Less.app, a free application that will compile your *.less* files into CSS every time you save the file (*http://incident57.com/less*). Simply keep the app (see Figure 15-1) open while you work, drag your theme's folder into it, and every time you save the file, it will compile your work into a .css file in the theme folder.

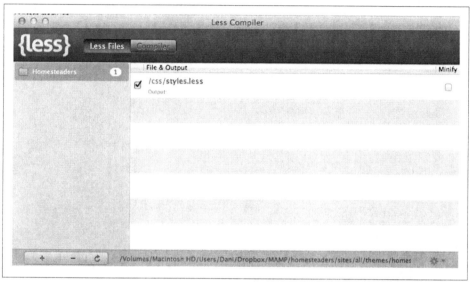

Figure 15-1. The handy Less.app "watches" any folder that you drag into it and compiles your LessCSS into CSS as you work

If you aren't on Mac (or you're working in OSX 10.5 or earlier—Less.app only works in 10.6 and above), there are other options for compiling your *.less* files:

The LessCSS Preprocessor module
> This module claims to process any *.less* file that you add to your theme's *.info* file (*http://drupal.org/project/less*). I've never used it before, so I can't vouch for how well it works; if you do have the ability to use Less.app, I'd use that before installing the module.

The Less.js JavaScript
> This JavaScript file (downloadable from *http://lesscss.org/* will process your *.less* files directly on the server if you include it in your theme's *.info* file.

Although both of these are perfectly fine options, I prefer using Less.app for one major reason: *I hate worrying about my JavaScript not running*. In an average Drupal installation, you're going to have quite a few *.js* files running on your site just because you installed Core and a couple of modules. Adding Less.js to the mix just adds another thing for the server to do when it serves up a page, and that adds weight to my site that I don't want to worry about. So if you can, I highly recommend using Less.app.

Working with LessCSS: Organizing Your Stylesheets

Confession: I'm hyper-organized when it comes to my CSS. Everything is ordered and numbered, with a table of contents. Call me OCD, but it works.

Whether I'm working in straight CSS or Less, every file starts about the same. Here, for example, is the table of contents for my Urban Homesteaders Unite theme:

```
/*
Custom styles for Urban Homesteaders Unite
Authors: Dani Nordin, tzk-design.com and Tricia Okin, papercutny.com

**Table of Contents**

1.0 Colors & Fonts
    1.1 Colors
    1.2 fonts
2.0 CSS3 Behaviors
3.0 Page Defaults
4.0 Navigation Menus
5.0 Drupal Defaults
6.0 Custom
7.0 Typography

*/
```

This way of organizing your CSS allows you to set up your page defaults near the top of the file, and put all your custom stuff at the bottom. This helps create a more natural flow as I'm theming; generally, I'll start by theming the Big Stuff (fonts, color standards, etc.), and then move into page-level or template-level variables. Note that I do include the main page typography at the bottom of the file; this ensures that any of my custom typography shows up *before* my global page typography, and get overridden.

Setting Up Color Variables

Before I switched to using LessCSS, I would incorporate color values into my table of contents. For example:

```
**Table of Contents**

Color Values:
gray: #8D8D7D;
dkgray: #4D4545;
```

```
mdgray: #666;
ltgray: #999;
palegray: #ccc;

red: #D32F00;
orange: #D17103;
cyan: #47A7BF;
green: #89A155;
gold: #eeb200;
```

That way, if I was in the middle of a big theming push, I could just do a quick "find" on the color I need by name and copy-paste it into what I was theming without having to remember the hex value. Now, with Less, I'm able to do the same thing, but instead of writing `color: #D32F00;` in my code, I can write `color: @red;` and Less.app will compile it into the CSS I need to make my object's text red. This means, in my `styles.less` file, I'll start myself off by defining those color variables:

```
/* 1.0 Colors & Fonts
            1.1 Colors */
@gray: #8D8D7D;
@dkgray: #4D4545;
@mdgray: #666;
@ltgray: #999;
@palegray: #ccc;

@red: #D32F00;
@orange: #D17103;
@cyan: #47A7BF;
@green: #89A155;
@gold: #eeb200;
```

After defining colors, I'll define the font mixins. LessCSS allows you to use entire bits of code as variables, called *mixins*. This is especially handy when working with CSS3 properties like rounded corners and drop-shadows (which usually require three lines of CSS). For my font mixins, I'm going to define some general defaults, using fonts that my partner Tricia and I have decided on:

```
/* 1.2 Fonts */

.serif-italic {
    font-family: 'ArvoItalic', Georgia, Times New Roman, serif;
}

.headings {
    font-family: 'ArvoRegular', Georgia, Times New Roman, serif;
    font-weight: normal;
}

.serif {
    font-family: Georgia, Times New Roman, serif;
}

.sans {
    font-family: 'PTSansRegular', Helvetica, Arial, san-serif;
```

```
    }

    .sans-italic {
        font-family: 'PTSansItalic', Helvetica, Arial, san-serif;
    }

    .caption-bold {
        font-family: 'PTSansBold', Helvetica, Arial, san-serif;
    }

    .caption-regular {
        font-family: 'PTSansCaptionRegular', Helvetica, Arial, san-serif;
    }

    .narrow-regular {
        font-family: 'PTSansNarrowRegular', Helvetica, Arial, san-serif;
    }
```

The use of the descriptors *.serif-italic*, *.serif*, and *.sans* is intentional; as the fonts may end up changing during the design phase, using generic descriptors like these allows me to change fonts site-wide simply by changing the font stack in a few lines of code. Less.app then compiles it to what I need. Using a generic name for the mixin also allows me to change the font without being tied to the name of the original font I chose. Now, let's say I wanted to change the headings in my site. I'd use the .headings variable as a line in my CSS, like so:

```
h1, h2, h3, h4 {
    .headings;
    color: @orange;
}
```

When Less.app outputs the CSS file, that will translate to:

```
h1,
h2,
h3,
h4 {
    font-family: 'ArvoRegular', Georgia, Times New Roman, serif;
    font-weight: normal;
    color: #d17103;
}
```

Brilliant, right? This is why I love using LessCSS. The next step is defining any CSS3 mixins I need. For this site, we're keeping things pretty low-key; the only thing we're really using is rounded corners for a few boxes here and there. For that, we'd put this in our code:

```
/* 2.0 CSS3 Variables */

.round-sm {
    /* all corners */
    -webkit-border-radius: 5px;
    -moz-border-radius: 5px;
    border-radius: 5px;
}
```

```
.round-lg {
    /* all corners */
    -webkit-border-radius: 10px;
    -moz-border-radius: 10px;
    border-radius: 10px;
}
```

Now, if we wanted to style everything with the class selector *button* to be green with rounded corners, we could add the following to our code:

```
/* Form elements */
.button {
    .serif-italic;

    a {
        color: white!important;
        .round-sm;
        background-color: @green;
        padding: 1em;
    }

    a:hover {
        background-color: @cyan;
    }
}
```

When it's compiled into CSS, I'll have something that looks like Figure 15-2.

Figure 15-2. Our lovely button

Why This is Awesome (Aside From the Obvious)

Aside from the sheer volume of code you can prevent yourself from having to write (your carpal tunnel will thank you), one of the things that makes LessCSS especially awesome when you're working in Drupal is the way it helps you organize your CSS according to parent/child relationships, which is essential to theming in Drupal.

In most cases, when theming Drupal elements, you'll be theming specific containers—say, all Views of a certain type, or a Featured Content block—and everything within those containers. In standard CSS, it's very easy to find yourself losing track of where you are in the hierarchy when you start getting into more complex relationships. This is especially true with navigation menus, where you have a multitude of selectors—and their immediate descendants—to deal with. But with LessCSS's nested styles, you can start from the top down and keep everything in one place. For example, here's the sample code from our *Event* page that we did in Chapter 11, *Prototyping in the Browser*:

```less
/* 6.2 Event Node */

.field-name-field-event-image {
    margin-bottom: 1em;
}



.about-host {
    .user-picture {
        float: left;
        margin-right: .5em;
    }

    h3 {
        margin: 0; padding: 0;
    }
    .username {
        font-size: 1em; line-height: 1.3em;
    }
}

.related-events {
    .views-row {
        margin: 1em 0;
        padding-bottom: .5em;
        border-bottom: 1px dotted @gray;
    }

    h4 {
        margin: 0; padding: 0;
    }

    .date {
        .sans-italic;
        font-size: .85em;
    }

}
```

Note that each block—*.about-host* and *.related-events*—starts off as its own thing, and all the elements that lie within those blocks are styled within the block. This not only helps you organize your code (no more will you end up with that handful of random styles thrown at the bottom of your stylesheet at the last minute), but it also helps you actually understand the parent-child relationships. Over time, I've been able to more easily figure out where my best top-level selector is—should I deal with the body of a page? The content area? A single block?—and create CSS that gives me the look I want to for a specific section of a theme without accidentally overriding CSS in other areas of the site.

Working with LessCSS on a Team

While there is much that is awesome about working with LessCSS, there is one minor sticking point. If you are working in LessCSS on a project that other people are contributing to, *each person on the team who is touching the CSS of the project must also be working in LessCSS.*

Although I've been able to figure it out with time, this has burned me a couple of times. Since LessCSS depends on being able to compile your *.less* files into *.css* files, anyone who wants to add to the styles of a given site needs to update the *.less* file, *not* the *.css* file, and compile that *.less* file into standard CSS code. If, for example, one of your colleagues decides to change or add CSS to the site, and they add it into *styles.css* (like many of us instinctively would), the moment that you go back into *styles.less* and make updates, *everything your colleague just wrote in styles.css would be overwritten when you compiled styles.less.*

If you're working on a project with a team—say you and another designer are working on a startup, and both of you will be theming the site—it's important to discuss this early on in the project. If possible, train them on how to use LessCSS syntax (it's really easy, once you get used to it) and point them to Less.app; if they can't use Less.app for whatever reason, consider adding *less.js* to your theme's *.info* file (make sure you download the *less.js* file to a folder called "js" in your theme folder as well), and let the server compile it for you.

About the Author

Dani Nordin is an independent user experience designer and strategist who specializes in smart, human-friendly design for progressive brands. She discovered design purely by accident as a Theatre student at Rhode Island College in 1995, and has been doing some combination of design, public speaking, and writing ever since.

Dani is a regular feature at Boston's Drupal meetup, and is a regular speaker at Boston's Design for Drupal Camp. In 2011, she was one of several contributors to *The Definitive Guide to Drupal 7*, published by Apress; she also authored *Planning and Managing Drupal Projects* for O'Reilly Media in 2011. *Design and Prototyping for Drupal* is her third book. You can check out some of her work at *tzk-design.com*. She also blogs almost regularly at *daninordin.com (http://daninordin.com)*.

Dani lives in Watertown, MA with her husband Nick and Persephone, a 14-pound ~~giant ball of black furry love~~ cat. Both are infinite sources of comedic gold.

Get even more for your money.

Join the O'Reilly Community, and register the O'Reilly books you own. It's free, and you'll get:

- $4.99 ebook upgrade offer
- 40% upgrade offer on O'Reilly print books
- Membership discounts on books and events
- Free lifetime updates to ebooks and videos
- Multiple ebook formats, DRM FREE
- Participation in the O'Reilly community
- Newsletters
- Account management
- 100% Satisfaction Guarantee

Signing up is easy:

1. Go to: oreilly.com/go/register
2. Create an O'Reilly login.
3. Provide your address.
4. Register your books.

Note: English-language books only

To order books online:
oreilly.com/store

For questions about products or an order:
orders@oreilly.com

To sign up to get topic-specific email announcements and/or news about upcoming books, conferences, special offers, and new technologies:
elists@oreilly.com

For technical questions about book content:
booktech@oreilly.com

To submit new book proposals to our editors:
proposals@oreilly.com

O'Reilly books are available in multiple DRM-free ebook formats. For more information:
oreilly.com/ebooks

O'REILLY®

Spreading the knowledge of innovators   oreilly.com

The information you need, when and where you need it.

With Safari Books Online, you can:

Access the contents of thousands of technology and business books

- Quickly search over 7000 books and certification guides
- Download whole books or chapters in PDF format, at no extra cost, to print or read on the go
- Copy and paste code
- Save up to 35% on O'Reilly print books
- **New!** Access mobile-friendly books directly from cell phones and mobile devices

Stay up-to-date on emerging topics before the books are published

- Get on-demand access to evolving manuscripts.
- Interact directly with authors of upcoming books

Explore thousands of hours of video on technology and design topics

- Learn from expert video tutorials
- Watch and replay recorded conference sessions

Spreading the knowledge of innovators   safari.oreilly.com